Writing
your
Nonfiction
Book

Trish Nicholson

Writing

your

Nonfiction

Book

Matador
9 Priory Business Park,
Wistow Road, Kibworth Beauchamp,
Leicestershire. LE8 0RX
Tel: (+44) 116 279 2299
Fax: (+44) 116 279 2277
Email: books@troubador.co.uk
Web: www.troubador.co.uk/matador

ISBN 978 1784620 660

British Library Cataloguing in Publication Data.
A catalogue record for this book is available from the British Library.

Typeset in 12pt Bembo by Troubador Publishing Ltd, Leicester, UK
Printed and bound in the UK by TJ International, Padstow, Cornwall

Matador is an imprint of Troubador Publishing Ltd

To the memory of Sylvia Taggart who found courage and gave love by writing.

Contents

'*A good head and good heart are always a formidable combination. But when you add to that a literate tongue or pen, then you have something very special.*'

Nelson Mandela

'*Either write something worth reading or do something worth writing.*'

Benjamin Franklin

'*I am of the firm belief that everybody could write books and I never understand why they don't.*'

Beryl Bainbridge

Introduction

Charles Dickens was a prolific author who understood the perils of procrastination. When we first meet Mr Dick, Miss Trotwood's eccentric lodger in *David Copperfield*, he has struggled for ten years to write his 'memorial'. By the end of the novel, some twenty years on, he is still struggling. It is too late for Mr Dick, but not for you.

I wrote *Writing Your Nonfiction Book* to inspire you and save you from Mr Dick's dilemma.

The only route to a successful book you can feel proud of – however it is published – is to produce the best possible manuscript you are capable of writing. Achieving this level of satisfaction requires commitment and hard work, but I will lead you, a step at a time, through the whole process, from your initial idea, to implementing options for publishing and marketing.

Everywhere, it seems, there is advice on how to write. What I've done differently here, is to focus on you, your subject and your reasons for writing about it, and to provide what you need to know in whichever corner of the world you happen to live, because with modern technology, everyone can write their book and participate successfully in the global market.

Writing Your Nonfiction Book is not a quick fix: there is no such method as a quick and easy way to produce a worthwhile book. Nor is there a one-size solution to constructing one, because nonfiction includes such a wide range of sub-genres and subjects. So, in addition to describing the techniques all nonfiction authors need to plan, research, and write, this guide includes detailed notes on structure and style for writing seven different genres:

- travelogues and guides
- history (including local history and family history)
- practical how-to books
- self-help

- memoir (including autobiography)
- biography
- educational and text books.

Enough scope here whether you intend to write on particle physics or brewing parsnip wine.

Reasons for writing a book vary as widely as the authors who create them, but passion, satisfaction and heritage usually figure somewhere among them. Because your own motivation influences what your book is about and how it is written, published and marketed, your purpose is the first question we consider at the beginning of Part One – Get it Together.

From that point, you follow the path that suits you best, because specific guidance is given whether your goal is to produce a handsome volume to distribute privately to family and friends, or you aim to take the market-place by storm and challenge Bill Bryson in the best sellers list. To achieve the latter, you must research the market. Trying to sell a book on a topic that has been written dry, or that no one wants to read about, is a hopeless task. That is why Part One steers you through the process of searching the market, identifying your readers and finding a unique angle for your book.

Planning and research are essential for nonfiction, so the remainder of Part One explains the construction of timelines, outlines and chapter summaries that give direction to data-gathering, and thread through the entire process until they feed into your marketing content. Chapter 4 deals with research. It explains types and sources of information, and how to validate them, in addition to creating your own primary data. In particular, I share a technique essential for all nonfiction writers: a smile-by-smile account of how to carry out a successful interview. And to keep you out of trouble, there is advice on recording your material to avoid problems with libel, liability and copyright.

Part Two – Get it Down – prepares you for constructing your first draft by delving into style, grammar, finding 'truth' and writing different genres. My focus is on narrative style, and the application of creative writing and storytelling techniques that readers and publishers now expect in works of nonfiction. Even writers of educational and text books on the driest subjects, can apply these tools to avoid producing tedious reading. People seek verifiable facts and sound research, but they also want to engage with subjects in ways that stimulate their imagination and emotions. Nonfiction writers who achieve this are the most successful, so we review the approaches of other authors, too.

Because I want to give you information and tips when you need them, and establishing a public presence as an author – an author platform – should begin well before a book is on the market, I explore initial steps in this long-term process in Chapter 6. The final chapter of Part Two pilots you through each stage of reviewing and self-editing your manuscript before accessing external feedback.

Part Three – Get it Out – untangles the confusing and constantly morphing process that leads to successful publication. After reviewing what current changes in publishing mean for you as an author with a new book to place, I explain the main options depending on the role you want to play: buying a full publishing package; selling publishing rights to a publisher; or publishing your book yourself. There are different costs and benefits involved with each option, and these are outlined to help you decide which role best achieves your goals.

The rest of Chapter 8 describes how to implement each of these options for print and digital publication. And as the emphasis in this guide is on practicality, detailed instructions are given on writing covering letters, queries, synopses and proposals, as well as critical aspects of designing a book cover, and where to obtain whatever technical assistance you might need if you decide to self-publish.

The final chapter covers a vital topic not often included in books on writing – how to market your book. One of the recent changes in publishing is that all authors, however they are published, must now participate in marketing and promoting their own work. For many writers, the market feels an alien and intimidating place, but it need not be so. Starting with the familiar – your own talents, your unique book, and the readers for whom you wrote it – I guide you through working out the most effective marketing strategy for your particular circumstances.

Marketing involves much more than 'selling' and is about identifying 'benefits' to customers, rather than pushing products. But no one set of methods suits everyone, so this chapter contains practical tips for setting up and using a wide range of promotional tools, such as social media, blogging, pitching, blurbs and tag-lines, press releases, launches, book reviews, and lots of ideas for longer-term on-going events and collaborations.

The Appendices include a list of useful books and websites that open up a wide range of related resources, and a glossary of common terms bandied about in writing, publishing and printing circles.

To gain the most benefit from this book, it is advisable to read it straight through first, to view the whole landscape and understand why topics are arranged the way they are – to offer exactly what you need at the right time. You will also appreciate how the work you accomplish at the start, feeds into later stages of your project. Knowing the road ahead, return to the beginning with confidence to take the first steps in your journey – it is an exciting expedition. Or as Terry Pratchett puts it: '*Writing is the most fun you can have by yourself.*'

I've worked hard to provide in this one place everything you need to write and publish a good nonfiction book. Even if you have written before, don't be tempted to skip stages and follow what you think are short-cuts. This is my seventh published nonfiction work, but as I draft *Writing Your Nonfiction Book*, I am following exactly the steps I share with you.

PART ONE

GET IT TOGETHER

1.

Pin Your Idea

What will you write about, why and for whom? You've obviously given it some thought already or you would not be here. And, no doubt, you know in general what you'd like to write, but vague intentions can drift for years unless you pin your idea down and determine why you are writing about a particular topic, and for whom. Who are your readers?

At this stage, these questions are more important than how you want to publish your work. Traditionally, for nonfiction, publishers asked for an outline of the book and a sample chapter, and made a decision on that basis because they expected to work with the author to develop the basic concept into a book that would fit their lists and the market. This is what an advance payment was for. When you submitted your proposal, you were not expected to offer a completed manuscript.

The benefit to authors was the assurance of publication and editorial assistance once their basic idea had been accepted, and their writing ability demonstrated by the sample chapter. But this is no longer the case with all publishers. Publishing has changed significantly even in the last five years. In particular, many publishers no longer consider a proposal unless a manuscript has already been completed, and advances are becoming rare, especially for 'unknown' authors. In any case, major publishers do not accept submissions direct from authors: you need an agent and they are almost harder to engage than a publisher.

One significant result of these changes, for you, is that this is not the only choice. The advent of digital technology has opened up entirely new pathways to publication; spawned different kinds of publishers and a range of ways to self-publish. These options are discussed in detail in a later chapter.

Why later and not now? – Because the most critical outcome of recent shifts in publishing is that, whichever route you choose, it is essential to start with the best manuscript you can produce on a subject that will interest people enough to want to buy it. Publishers are in the business of selling books. They will only invest time and money in a book they are convinced people will want to read. If you self-publish, you will need to adopt a similar business approach if you want your book to be financially successful.

It is not necessary at this point to decide how you want your book published. Aim high: you can always adjust your sights later, if necessary. If you limit your vision before you start, it is harder to expand horizons.

Defining your subject and readers:

Maybe you've completed the trip of a lifetime; survived an extraordinary experience; possess expertise in a particular subject; or wish to record your family history. Even if you intend your book to be shared only with family and friends, you will still want that written heritage to be the best you can write.

The first step is to clarify your purpose, because that will be your main motivation to sustain you through this lengthy adventure. To help your thinking, some of the reasons why people write a nonfiction book are to:

- Share with others their passion for a particular subject
- Leave a personal record for family, friends and posterity
- Correct the record of events or issues with new facts or insights
- Enable others to benefit from their specialist knowledge and expertise
- Disseminate a message they feel is of wide and urgent public interest
- Increase their professional credibility in a subject to further their career
- Apply the book as a promotional and marketing tool to boost their business
- Support and publicise a charitable cause

- Generate income – a tiny percentage achieve it but there are easier ways
- Enjoy the challenge and satisfaction of doing so

Mull over your aims for a while and make a few notes of your thoughts and conclusions.

Next, identify your potential readers by age range and general characteristics: students, hobbyists, the actively retired, small business owners, nature-lovers, general readers, and so on. The audience you aim for will affect what you say and how you say it – how much previous knowledge or experience you expect of readers, for example – so you should think about this now. It will also determine how the book is marketed later.

Jot down a brief description of the sort of people you want to read your book. What would they expect? What would they most like to know about? Where would you find them?

Finally, you need to be aware in which genre you will be writing. The thousands of titles published each year are categorised according to genres, i.e. their content and approach. The major divide is between fiction and nonfiction, but within nonfiction, books are further differentiated, for example, into travelogues, histories, memoirs, biographies, practical and business how-to books, self-help guides (including 'mind, body and spirit'), food and wine, science and other educational topics, or commentaries on current issues.

You may think your idea does not fit neatly into a category – it is, after all, uniquely yours – but it is important to understand genres because that is the way both the physical and digital book trade is organised. Think of it as an array of stalls at the market: on which stall will your book be noticed by customers who congregate there because it displays the sort of books they like to read?

A small kiosk in a corner of the market hall might contain a collection of specialised books for devotees of a certain topic – what is called a niche market – but it is necessary to scout for potential customers to let browsers know you are there. Niche books depend on tightly focused and highly effective marketing.

To develop a better idea of genres and to identify your own, look on the shelves of a good bookshop to see what sort of books are in which sections, and search online bookstores and publishers' websites.

I suggest starting with The Book Depository because their website design provides a calm experience for researching and it is extremely easy to find your way around. This link www.thebookdepository.com opens onto the HOME page. Look at the column on the left which is a long list of categories (all are nonfiction except for the one listing of 'fiction' which takes browsers to a different section). Select your subject and browse the books that appear. For those closest to your topic, read the descriptions to gain an idea of content, and look at a few reviews to see what readers like and dislike about them. Note that The Book Depository lists only books that are in print form, so investigate a range of other online retail sites for ebooks, not only Amazon, but also those that serve your country.

Sometimes a classification is not clear cut: 'travel memoir' for example. But if your book is based on your experience in a particular location – working in Tuscany, say – includes detailed descriptions of the region and inhabitants, as well as how they affected you, then you can slant it to attract readers of travel; if you wish to aim at readers of memoir, it would focus more on you, with the location being simply part of the context. Memoir is fashionable at the moment (especially those of celebrities), but travel is a larger market and probably less prone to shifting tastes.

Similarly with a biography of a historical figure: although you would place them in the social context of the period, if your account focuses primarily on that person and their entire life, it is biography rather than history.

And I notice that 'autobiography' tends to be listed under 'biography' in online stores. This is misleading because there are significant differences I will discuss shortly, but you will find most modern autobiographies in the 'biography' category.

Thinking around genres:

Travel – the range of content and style is surprisingly large:

- Guidebooks, normally quite short, may provide information on every aspect of a location, or specialise on certain features – e.g. 'the best beaches in New Zealand' – but they require meticulous research, and shelf-life is shorter because details become out of date. Depending on the purpose of a guide, it may also contain historical and geographical background.

• Travelogues (sometimes referred to as 'travel narratives') focus on a single trip like a trek, a train journey, a canoeing holiday, or extol the virtues of an island or a whole country in greater depth and with more 'story' than a guide book, including the author's experiences and reflections. They tend to form two main approaches: the 'good life' of food, wine and romance, and the 'adventure' of sailing across an ocean, scaling a mountain, or exploring a little known area. The main emphasis, though, is on the journey and/or the location.

• Travel memoir focuses more strongly on the author's feelings and relationships and usually, but not always, recounts longer experience. For example, the author's work or life in a particular location, or emigration to another country. People and places encountered are important to the story, but reflections and conclusions of broader significance are expected in this sub-genre.

History – a similarly wide choice of focus and breadth:

• A general history describes events during a specified period – for example, the reign of a particular monarch; the 18th century; or the years between the two World Wars. It is not easy to cover all aspects of society in one study and requires extensive research. Unless you access previously unpublished material that provides an entirely fresh interpretation of events, it may be difficult to compete with what is already published, but many 'post-colonial' countries have yet to write their own histories and there is a lot of scope in that area.

• A focused history narrows the field to a deeper exploration of one aspect of a period or event – the Victorian's preoccupation with murder, for example, which has already been written. Research may be especially demanding because of the detail required, but the scope is limited only by what would interest a wide audience of readers.

(Be aware that the reason a subject is neglected in books may be that few people wish to read about it).

- The lives of ordinary people are often neglected in older general histories, especially those of women and the poor. Both are more topical now and could be worth investigating; other possibilities are changes in a particular industry; in transport; science; a product – beer, for example – and the history of a particular idea, of cigarette smoking, fashion, musical instruments, or even teddy bears.

- Local histories – their potential as a topic depends on what your locality has to offer. Local histories obviously appeal to a smaller market, but most people in the area will want to read it and, depending on the location, it might be sufficiently attractive to visitors to be stocked by local museums, bookshops, hotels and visitor centres.

- Extended local histories – another way to broaden the interest is to relate local history to national or international affairs or prominent people, if there is scope for this. Perhaps a local railway line has some special feature of potential interest to rail enthusiasts anywhere, or a historical event of national significance took place in the town.

- Family history – probably for self-publishing or private circulation. Although a family history is a closely-centred form of history, in many respects it is close to memoir, and is unlikely to be taken up by a publisher. I include it here because the research and planning are similar to any other history. The potential market can also be broadened by identifying any special characteristics of family members and their actions that have, or had, wider implications. And one way to gain universal appeal is to make it funny – everyone loves a laugh – but writing humour requires a great deal of skill and, presumably, peculiar relatives.

Memoir, autobiography and biography:

- A memoir is not about an entire life from birth to death (that is autobiography). Instead, it is a noteworthy slice of a life, the period covered depending on the key episode or relationship that forms its focus. Sometimes an author's significant other – parent, partner, child or friend – has as large a role as the author in the story because of the impact of their relationship. Your memoir may share a period of your life, or that of someone close to you.

- Memoirs have been written about journeys, about recovering from illness, or surviving some cataclysmic event like an earthquake, and they involve places and other people as well as the author. They also include reflections and conclusions on the meaning of the experience. While memoirs of the less-famous are difficult to place with agents and publishers, they are sometimes successfully written to fit a genre with a wider market, such as travel and self-help books.

- Autobiographies recount an entire life, but obviously, not *everything* that happened. Selection is critical in revealing personality as well as achievements and failures. Although place and other people clearly play a role, the individual is the core of an autobiography. Unless you are already a public figure, or have led a truly exceptional life, it is unlikely that your autobiography would be published by anyone but yourself. But this is no reason not to write one, whatever your life story. It can be an enriching experience and a heritage to leave for others.

- Biographies also cover an entire life, but someone else's, so how much can be written about that person depends on what original documents and private papers are available. If a biography has already been written about your subject, you would have to find new material or a new interpretation of existing information to make your book unique. If no one has written about them before, ask yourself why not: perhaps they are not sufficiently interesting to enough readers.

- A biography also includes a social history of the time in which the person lived, but it should be woven into their story and balanced, or the account may become a history rather than a biography.

How-to and self-help books – success depends on picking the right topic:

- 'How-to' is a phrase so loved by internet search engines that you can capitalise on the fact in the titles of books normally in other categories: 'How to Travel on a Pension' for a travel guide, or 'How to Do Your Homework' for an educational book on study methods. The range of topics encompasses every field of human endeavour, although money, health and happiness figure prominently. Researching what is already published is essential.

- Practical how-to books can be about any skill, from making matchstick models to starting a llama farm. Choice of subject depends on your knowledge and expertise for which you will be required to demonstrate credibility. The main question is: How many people would want to know? 'How to Make a Fast Buck' will have wider appeal than 'How to Repair Old Books', but popular subjects will already be published. If yours is, search for some fresh approach or new technique.

- Self-help books range from guidance written by experts on medical or psychological conditions, for example, to advice based on shared experience such as bereavement, divorce, changing a career, or leading a fuller, happier life. It is a growing genre and books are usually short, but success can be short-lived as each new solution to life is nudged out of the way by the next.

- Writing about shared experience is close to memoir and a detailed, well-informed and well-written account of living successfully with dyslexia, dementia or Asperger's Syndrome, for example – all of which affect large numbers of people – might contain wider appeal as an engaging memoir, and help many more readers.

Text books and educational books:

- Educational books cover any field of learning and are often directed at the interested general reader as well as students: 'popular science' and 'popular history' categories, for example. The difference to other books on a particular subject is that teaching is the main purpose. This influences the way information is presented: educational books include a bibliography, appendices, end notes and, possibly, study guidance and questions.

- A text book can cover any field that is taught in an educational establishment, and is usually written by someone teaching that subject. Text books are a specialised field of publishing and requirements differ according to curricula in different countries.

- Unless you are connected to an institution likely to publish your book – a university press, for example – this is one genre for which you should contact publishers before you complete the manuscript. They may, for example, list a series to which you could contribute, in which case you would follow closely their editorial instructions regarding content and approach. Depending on subject, text books can be listed for many years, but it is a finite market and the main benefit for an author may be professional, rather than financial.

- Despite these special conditions, I include text books here because the current trend is increasingly to write even academic books in a more narrative style – easier to read and less detached from the reader. To write for educational purposes these days, you need not only up-to-date subject knowledge, but the skill to engage and stimulate a reader's imagination through the written word (skills explained in Chapter 5).

Finding your spot in the market:

Once you've identified your genre, keep searching to see what else is written on your subject. Click on the 'Look Inside' feature in online bookstores to see what each book covers and how the material is organised; download free samples and read them, making a note of titles you might want to read fully later.

Look for ideas on how to approach your project, but note especially what is already published so that you can find a different angle for your own book. As you examine the market for your topic, ask yourself:

- Is a particular area, time period, perspective or technique, not covered?
- Is a book listed as part of a series to which you could contribute?
- Are existing titles out of date?
- Is there a type of reader that is not catered for?
- What will be uniquely special about *your* book?

To check what local histories and guides are already available in your area, talk to staff at the library, museum and tourist information office.

There is no point in writing a book about a topic with an approach that is already published: that pitch in the market-place is already taken. You must find a spot of your own with an original angle on the subject. When I made this type of search the other day, I found the following titles with an innovative perspective on their genres:

Deep Sea and Foreign Going by Rose George (published by Portobello) is an ethnographic travelogue of people involved in container shipping. The author joined a massive container ship on a long sea voyage to investigate the effects on the crew of this rapidly expanding trade, and carried out further research on environmental and wider social outcomes. The travel aspect encompasses a global economic trend and relates this to the lives of individuals the author interviewed during her sea journey. She also shows its relevance to our daily lives.

What Jane Austen Ate and Charles Dickens Knew by Daniel Pool (Touchstone) contains factual history with a slant towards fiction. The items selected for inclusion are those that readers of nineteenth century English novels need to understand in order to gain the most from their reading. It includes an explanation of 'the ague' and the social intricacies of 'calling cards', as well as how social and political institutions of the times operated. Although the style is humorous, the research is thorough and the last third of the book is an annotated glossary of words or phrases, citing in which novels they are significant.

The Poets' Daughters: Dora Wordsworth and Sara Coleridge by Katie

Waldegrave (Hutchinson) offers fresh biographical points of view on the lives of two poets already much written about, by focusing on the close relationship between their daughters. The two families lived not far from each other in the English Lake District and their lives were intertwined. Both daughters played significant roles in their respective fathers' literary careers by editing, copying, or writing accompanying notes, and both acted as guardians of the poets' literary legacies. More books are published about Coleridge and Wordsworth than perhaps any other poets, but *The Poets' Daughters* provides an entirely fresh perspective on their lives.

Mongol by Uuganaa Ramsay (Saraband Books) is a memoir which recounts the author's early life in Mongolia. When she moves to the UK and her baby son is diagnosed with Down's Syndrome, she discovers that the word 'mongol' has a different, and offensive, meaning in the West. She has to cope with this stigma and superstition as well as grief after Billy's death. Through this experience, she gains the strength to champion a public understanding of this medical condition as nothing to do with being Mongolian. Although the book is a memorial to Billy, it is not a tirade of advocacy; instead, these issues are woven into her story of personal transformation.

Tie-dye: Dye it, Wear it, Share it by Shabd Simon-Alexander (Potter Craft), a practical how-to book, describes the ancient techniques of tie-dying step-by-step, but does so from the perspective of its modern relevance in fashion, and details twenty-five different project ideas for applying it. When I saw it, it was high on The Book Depository's sales ranking. Potter Craft is a small press specialising in a wide range of craft and DIY titles; a useful possibility for craft writers. (Potter Craft is part of the Crown Publishing Group which is now an imprint of the Penguin Random House conglomerate.)

The Kiwi Backyard Handbook by Justin Newcombe (Penguin Group NZ) is not so much innovative in content as closely targeted to the New Zealand market, in particular, the do-it-yourself culture, and the popularity of gardening and outdoor magazines. His book contains twenty-five step-by-step practical projects for starting a garden and enhancing the backyard with useful structures. The layout is similar to a magazine, with every page illustrated with colour photographs of the author completing each step.

How to Get a Grip: (Forget Namby-Pamby, Wishy Washy, Self-Help Drivel. This is the Book You Need) by Matthew Kimberley (Ad Lib, a private printing press). The author has written a self-help book with the unique approach of bucking the trend in this genre, aiming to appeal to a wider market. It is described in the advertising blurb as: '*the self-help manual for people who hate self-help*', and covers a broad range of issues including career, personal relationships and health. Although a self-published book with an extraordinarily long – but provocative – title, it was selling well on The Book Depository, presumably attracting readers who would not normally buy a self-help book.

17 Equations that Changed the World by Ian Stewart (Profile Books) provides an accessible and popular text book on algebra by explaining the significance of these equations to our social history. In a series of 'stories', he describes, for example, how Pythagorus led us to GPS systems and the development of SatNav, the role logarithms play in architecture, and so on, through all seventeen equations. An unusually entertaining approach to mathematics, this book is listed as a best seller.

The way you approach this stage depends on your reasons for writing a book: if you want it to be financially successful, researching and responding to the market is essential; if you have a yen to write about repairing old books, you will need to search out the niche market where others are passionate about old books, too. Or, you can write for the sheer joy of writing and the love of your subject, accepting that the number of people who read it will be limited. The choice is yours, but you do need to make one, so that you can lay the right foundations.

You may find it helpful to discuss your idea with someone else – a colleague, friend, or a potential source of information – but a word of warning: think carefully about who you should approach. For whatever reason, others may be discouraging, unintentionally or otherwise, or their attitude towards the topic may lead you from your own path. Initial book ideas are delicate creatures and must be handled with care and respect. It is better at this stage to ask in more general terms about the subject and what is available, which may also reap suggestions on unmet needs for information.

And beware of 'talking the book out' – speaking about your ideas so often and fully that you drain them from your head and the talking replaces the writing. Keep a notebook handy and jot down ideas and thoughts as they come to you for later review, rather than dissipate them by discussing them too early. Later, with a firm plan and your first draft, you will be in a stronger position to benefit from others' comments and consider them more critically.

What to do now:

→   Once you've done some searching and thinking around your idea, write three short paragraphs to state clearly and specifically each of the following: your overall purpose; your potential readers and what benefit they gain from reading your book; the genre of your book and how you will make it different to other works on that topic. Print it out and stick it on the wall.

It is important to be clear on your general destination, but remember, this is not chiselled into granite – don't let it become your headstone. One of the wonderful aspects of writing with modern technology is the flexibility of the process; the ease with which we can add, edit or correct what we write. Your ideas will develop as you carry out further research and write your first draft, so will your skills. You can review where you're heading and make adjustments as you progress.

There are no mistakes, only small exploits that may or may not produce what you wanted for this specific project. Keep everything: nothing in writing is wasted.

→   Read as much as you can of your genre before you start. Make brief notes on each book like the examples above, (you will also be accumulating a useful list of publishers).

→   Read reviews in newspapers and magazines, as well as online, to become aware of what critics and readers consider 'good' about nonfiction books.

You will need to read for research throughout the writing of your book, but whether you continue with background reading of your genre is a matter of personal confidence. If you fear undue influence from someone else's style, or find yourself tempted to copy what they write, it might be better not to. Just something you should think about.

2.

Make Your Plan

I f you have written any fiction, or heard writers talk about their work, you might already be familiar with the 'pantsers' versus 'plotters' debate. 'Pantsers' swing straight into writing 'by the seat of their pants' without prior planning on the basis that this allows creativity to flow unrestricted. This method requires major edits and several re-writes of the first draft. 'Plotters' lay out the plot and critical sequences to guide them before they start, although the plan will not be followed rigidly. In fiction, it's a matter of personal choice as to which system suits an individual writer. In nonfiction, 'pantsing' does not work.

Although you will apply creative writing craft and story techniques to enhance your manuscript (covered in detail in chapter 5), nonfiction writers must follow logical steps; keep track of sources and references, and check the accuracy of what they write. You need a plan.

If you decide to submit your manuscript to agents or publishers, they will ask for a proposal, which includes the genre, purpose and potential readers (you noted these already); an outline of each chapter, and a synopsis. But don't wait until that stage: you need the framework in front of you as you write.

Because people often confuse a synopsis with an outline – thinking they are the same thing – it is a good idea to clarify the difference before we start. An outline indicates the main topics that will be included in a manuscript; how they are arranged into separate chapters and sections, and the order in which they are presented. In appearance, it is similar to a table of contents, but with brief descriptions of the key features in each chapter, and how one links to the next.

A synopsis is a compact piece of text – around 300 words – through which an author provides an overall impression of a book by selecting the essential elements to show how the idea is developed and concluded. It is written in the same style as the main manuscript. You can think of it as a miniature experience of the book. Imagine looking through the wrong end of a telescope: you can't see all the details, but you appreciate the basic shape, pattern and colour.

Obviously, the synopsis is best written when the first draft is complete – we come to that in a later chapter – but the outline is your essential starting point to guide your research as well as your writing. It also allows the creative freedom to work on any chapter you wish, depending on the material or inspiration available at the time, because you always know exactly where you are in the outline.

Your outline is not etched on steel – it will develop with revisions and additions as you complete your research and work your way through the manuscript – but it is the SatNav to keep you on the right road. Putting effort into this preparatory stage is the best investment you will make in your book. It saves time and avoids errors in all subsequent stages.

The three steps to follow are: compiling a timeline; determining the theme of your book, and creating the outline structure.

Compiling a timeline:

A timeline is a list of key dates and events in chronological order. Accurate dates are essential for history, biography and memoir; for travel, routes and locations might be more significant, and for how-to books, a timeline focuses on the sequence of steps or instructions to be followed in a process. Even if time and sequences seem less relevant to your subject, you still need to list topics and issues to be covered and put them in some kind of order: that is what the timeline achieves.

Do some preliminary research and brainstorming – the list should be as full as possible to give you plenty of ideas to work with. Your book will not necessarily be written in exactly this order, but the timeline has several valuable functions:

• It sets down briefly the events relevant to the topic to give you an overall view, making it easier to prioritise what to include and what to omit.

- It enables you to assess whether or not your list is complete and where there might be gaps, and if you think of other things later, it is easy to add them in the right place.

- You have a quick, accurate reference tool as you write – this is the time to double-check details before possible errors become embedded in your text.

- As an option, you can include in the timeline a note of references you need to access, or people to be interviewed. I find this helpful to forward-plan my research, especially for information that might take time to acquire.

- The timeline can form the basis of a simplified chronology for an appendix to your book, if that is necessary.

- It builds the foundation for working out your theme, and then your outline.

A useful tip is to construct your timeline as a table with three columns, listing the events or issues in one, research to be accessed in the second, and notes on progress in the third. It is a working document that will be updated as you progress. But if that sounds too complicated at this stage, a simple list will suffice.

The important thing is to make your timeline as comprehensive as possible. You may not include everything from the list in your book, but this is your foundation. It will inspire as well as guide you, and small details could provide excellent examples or lighter moments in the final text.

Print out the timeline and pin that to the wall, too, or at least keep it on the desk for easy reference. You will add to it or adjust it as you work through the research later.

Determining your theme:

The theme is the slant, the angle, the perspective from which you share the knowledge and experience you write about. It will be related to your purpose, but is more than that. Every piece of writing needs a theme, which may or may not be explicitly expressed, but is reflected in its content and in the author's selection of words and images.

You should think about this now because the theme determines what you research, and the way you look at your material and assess your priorities – giving more space to some issues than others, or describing certain places in more detail – and deciding the order in which to present information.

Read through the timeline to remind yourself of the whole 'story' and reflect on the main reason you want to explain it – the message you want to share – that will lead you to your theme. It could provide the clue to what makes your book unique among others in the same genre.

Theme can be an elusive concept to grasp initially, so here are a few examples:

- A scientist whose purpose is to stimulate public interest in her area of study could select the theme: how the ordinary gives rise to the extraordinary. The focus of the book might then be the personal stories of unsung heroes in science and the discoveries they made. This would guide the research and selection of material to be included.

- Someone who had spent time overseas, perhaps as a volunteer worker, and gained insights into environmental or development problems, might want to share his passion. The theme for his travel narrative could be: development transforms peoples' lives in unpredictable ways. The book would focus on local peoples' experiences in their geographical setting, with perhaps an introduction on the main issues involved.

- A writer of a business book aiming to encourage others to start small ventures might identify a particular section of the population for a theme: active retirees can make additional income, for example. In that case, the book would address the problems of credit for older people, the risks in re-mortgaging property for working capital and other related concerns, as well as general tips on business acumen.

- As a memoir does not cover the whole of a life, but revolves around a particular experience and how this affected the author and the people associated with her, these events provide your theme. The experience could involve an illness, a relationship, or a journey – themes for any of these could be: we don't know our inner strength until it is challenged, or, acceptance and perseverance work in tandem.

Theme runs like a fine thread woven through the book. It may be explicitly stated in the introduction and/or the ending, or simply 'there' as a subtle presence, but without a theme, a book lacks cohesion and a sense of purpose; it becomes a dull series of facts or happenings leaving the reader wondering why it was written.

In the popular history *Medieval Lives* (BBC Books), authors Terry Jones and Alan Ereira set out to correct the common misconception that the medieval period in Europe – the 'Middle Ages' – was a time of unrelieved ignorance, squalor and doom. This is their theme. To achieve it, they research and describe the life and livelihoods of eight different 'occupational' groups – peasant, minstrel, outlaw, monk, philosopher, knight, damsel and king – and weave into these daily details the facts that prove their point. For example, an archaeological dig in a rural village revealed the skeleton of a man with a head injury that had been surgically treated; successfully so, because he had recovered, dying some years later from other causes.

The theme determines not only the content of *Medieval Lives*, but emerges in its structure – the form in which the material is organised and presented. The 'characters' and their stories echo the motley collection of pilgrims who set out together, and entertain each other along the way, in *The Canterbury Tales* written by Geoffrey Chaucer, himself one of the most memorable characters of the Middle Ages.

In *Deep Sea and Foreign Going* mentioned earlier, the theme – that the shipping-container trade is not only a huge international affair economically, but has global social and environmental effects – guided the questions the author asked in interviews, and the data bases she consulted for statistical information.

In her recent book *Conversations With my Sons and Daughters* (Penguin Global), South African social and political activist, Mamphela Ramphele, takes as her theme the disillusionment of young South Africans, and how cross-generational understanding can help them to retrieve and realise the dream of a just and open post-apartheid society.

Our experiences, memories and knowledge are not neutral; what we notice, how we interpret and decide to write about it – and the theme we choose – are based on our own values. Writing a book shares your vision; it is an expression of your voice as a person.

Having the theme in your mind enables you to 'highlight', mentally, or actually, your material for what is most relevant, and guides you in constructing the outline of your book.

Creating your chapter outline:

The chapter outline defines the structure which leads readers through the subject of your book. It's like the design of a building – an exhibition centre for example – where a foyer might contain some announcements, or reveal highlights of the event, and then direct you through a door to the first room. Here, discreet signs might guide you through the exhibits in a particular order before drawing you along to the next room, and the next; there may be stairs, passages, corners and other doorways to all the other rooms, until you end up at the cafeteria with a well-earned coffee and cake while you think about your experience.

The route through your book should be logical – don't leave readers stranded on the first floor landing or accidentally trapped in a broom cupboard – but the journey needs variety in content and pace, with points of excitement and places for reflection, and so does the substance of each chapter.

And size does matter. Unless you are writing for a series of mini-books or guides, for example, (which might be any length from 10,000 words to 30,000), the usual minimum word count for nonfiction paperback books is 40,000-60,000 words. Anything less and the production costs per book become disproportionate to the price readers are willing to pay. Publishers also like at least a 0.5cm width spine to print the title and author in a font large enough to be read from the shelf by bookshop customers.

Typing on A4 page size, double spaced with normal margins (2.54cms) and using 12pt Times New Roman font, 60,000 words would amount to approximately 160 pages. Many books are longer than this, up to 100,000 words, especially for history, travelogue or biography, but publishers are wary of manuscripts much beyond that length. The number of pages in a final printed book will depend on its width of margins, font size and style, and overall dimensions.

Digital production costs are lower (though not the fees for professional editing, indexing and proofreading) and ebooks can be any length. No longer are writers pressured to pad out their text to fill a publishers' requirement for a minimum spine width. The value of strong, concise writing at its natural length is receiving more recognition, in Amazon's Kindle Singles and Collca's BiteSize series, for example. There is ample scope to break down a large collection of material into a series of short digital books, each 15,000-25,000 words – a more achievable goal for many first-time authors and much easier to have published.

Most print books are also available in digital formats these days, although a book of practical instructions might be handier in print form than on a screen. However, if you want to show illustrations and photographs, they are expensive to print and the number you could include is likely to be limited, whereas the lower costs of digital publication allows you as many as you wish.

To get the feel of book sizes, look through books in your genre to see how they are laid out, and how many pages they contain. Make a rough estimate of how many pages and chapters might be required for your subject.

With your theme at the back of your mind, examine the timeline carefully and work out which events need a whole chapter; how you could chunk others together, and whether some information should come first to make sense of later chapters. Chapter length can vary: the first couple might be quite short – 1,000-2,000 words each – with later chapters being 5-6,000. And short chapters might act as links from one part of a topic to another, for example. But each chapter, and the book as a whole, should be balanced, so all the interesting parts don't bulge out at the beginning and fizzle out to nothing before you reach the end.

Think back to your readers. What kind of read would they expect? Are they devotees who would want a deep read of a favourite subject? An in-depth study of some facet of sport, music, or history, for example, might demand fewer, longer chapters delving into all aspects connected with the topic, perhaps with subheadings. Or is your audience seeking an easy-read reference of many brief ideas, or a basic introduction to a subject? A book containing forty ways to make an extra dollar will comprise at least forty short, snappy sections and probably lots of bullet points.

What you are looking for in your outline is a logical progression that maintains readers' interest without confusing them by switching time, place or subject too violently.

The simplest structure is chronological – a linear time progression from the start to the finish. For a practical how-to book, you would need to apply this structure for describing the steps to be followed in a process. But a self-help book on taking up a new life-style, for example, might start at the end by showing some of the benefits gained, then go on to explain the situation 'before'.

Whatever outline you construct, the book should start with impact to compel the reader to keep turning the pages. The first chapter might recount some dramatic episode that has wide repercussions later in the book, and then in the next chapter, draw the reader in to learn how it all started. That first bit of drama acts as a 'hook': arousing the reader's curiosity to read further. This story technique can be used for almost any subject.

A chapter might be needed that is out of sequence, that digresses to an earlier or a future period, or to a side issue which needs to be disclosed before you can move on to the next part of the narrative. This is called a 'flashback' (or 'flash forward'); used sparingly, they can create variety of pace and content, but they must be clearly 'signposted' before and afterwards: readers have been known to get lost in flashbacks, never to be seen again.

Below are some possibilities to consider for each genre. These are more complex structures which may appear challenging, but they suggest potential for an original approach and it is worth considering whether they would allow you to explore your subject fully. Sketch an idea out roughly, if it doesn't work – because the right kind of data is not available, for example – you can always return to a simpler outline.

Whatever your genre, I recommend you read the whole section: inspiration comes from unexpected directions.

Ideas for structuring different genres:

Travel:

Above all, a travel guide must be clear and logical to follow. Describing country walks would follow each path and route, describing the terrain and what to look out for. A more general guide of an area could be divided into places of interest, accommodation, where to eat and so on, with subheadings. But travelogues offer wide possibilities for structure.

A trek or a long train or sea journey might best be described chronologically, one day at a time, weaving in adventures along the way, but in the gaps where nothing much happens for several days, (which is often the case on such trips), intervening chapters might reflect on the country, the journey and life in general, providing variety of content and pace.

For other activities, regardless of the route you actually travelled, a country can be described by starting at the coast and working inland; from a river estuary to the watershed and vice versa; from a cold region to a hot one, or you might structure your account to follow the trail of a famous, earlier traveller and make comparisons with what he or she observed.

If your travelogue is based on a year or more in a particular location, you could divide your material into chapters according to the four seasons; or into four parts as an overall framework, arranging shorter chapters within each.

A travelogue themed on the 'good life' and exploring the food and wine of a region as well as other activities, might be based for its overall structure on the notion of a dinner menu: an early chapter of 'pre-dinner nibbles' describing your initial impressions; 'the entree' detailing short trips and snack food; a 'main course' with deeper portrayal of your principal destination and major entertainments it offers, including restaurants, and so on through dessert, coffee and mints or however many 'courses' you need to tell your travel tale.

A book about a city may not involve much travel, but if it is renowned for some product – silk weaving, glass blowing, carpet making – or for a famous artist or founding hero, the logic of the account could follow the processes of production, or the life of the hero, revealing facts, places, events, architectural features and significant people at each stage. In the French city of Lyon – the centre of silk weaving in the 15th century – visible clues to the city's past and present are evident in the covered stone alleys *(traboules),* through which silk weavers carried bolts of fabric to keep them safe from the weather. One silk producer remains, bringing the story up to date.

If you are lucky enough to spend time with a family in another country, you could – with their permission – structure your narrative around that family's story, expanding from the particular to the general in showing the culture and surroundings in which they live: a wedding, for example, reveals a great deal about relationships and customs, as well as descriptions of location. For an example of this, read Asne Seierstad's *The Bookseller of Kabul* (Virago), where she portrays society under the Taliban, and the forms of resistance people adopted, through an intimate portrait of a bookseller and his family.

Histories and biographies:

Histories and biographies are likely to be based, overall, on a chronology of events, but other possibilities within that general arc are worth thinking about, depending on the amount and type of information available. If you have access to diaries and correspondence, chapters could be written from the perspective of different key people involved, each building up the 'story', with other chapters providing historical context and tying it all together. This structure suits family histories where living members are able to give their own stories, while the author provides the framework and feeds in background data from other research.

If several interesting locations are involved, and important in the theme, chapters might be divided according to place, with descriptions that weave into the account their influence on events that happened there.

A history of a particular profession, or craft – pottery, for example – might follow the life stages of a potter, and through that, expand on wider aspects of the craft, the materials, products and trade. Similarly, the phases of constructing a manor house or the laying out of a 16th century ornamental garden, can act as signposts to explore related matters that gradually build up the wider history of an area or period. These structures are called 'framing devices' and, once you start to think about them, the possibilities are limitless.

Similar frames can work for biographies. But even a simple chronological biography can avoid the monotony of a life divided evenly into decades. Each chapter might concentrate on a phase of life: if your subject's teenage years were significant, those might be in a 'coming of age' chapter. A period of travel or uncertainty might be the 'wanderer' chapter, and a particularly traumatic event lasting only a weekend might require an entire chapter of its own.

If the circumstances of birth are especially interesting, that could make a dramatic beginning, but it is not necessary to start with their birth, or even their parents. If their death was mysterious or otherwise remarkable, begin with that, perhaps giving only part of the story, revealing the rest at the end when you've revealed the life that led up to it.

Peter Ackroyd employs this approach in his biography of Edgar Allan Poe, *Poe: a Life Cut Short* (Vintage). The first chapter relates the mysterious circumstances of Poe's death; the second narrates the lives of his parents with a suggestion that their lifestyle and poverty influenced Poe's character and the subsequent difficulties of his life, even before his birth. An idea supported by a quote from Poe: '*I do believe God gave me a spark of genius but He quenched it in misery.*' In the final chapter we learn of Poe's last year of life and the rest of the story of his death.

An interesting combination of history and biography is found in *The History of Tibet – Conversations with the Dalai Lama,* by Thomas Laird (Atlantic). The fourteen chapters are chronological, beginning with Tibet's pre-history, and obviously required a great deal of historical research, but its interpretation is largely through the eyes of the Fourteenth Dalai Lama, based on eighteen personal interviews with him spread over three years. Approximately a third of the book focuses on events during his incumbency up until 2006, when the account was concluded and published. The final chapter is an Epilogue, in which the Dalai Lama has the last word in the form of a long letter to the author.

Memoir and autobiography:

Although an entire lifespan forms the arc of an autobiography, and some events may need to be established before later developments can be understood, there are more interesting and creative ways of describing your life than plodding stolidly from year to year.

Your life and character can be revealed through special events – personal or social – that affected you, or key people who influenced you for good or ill. The same applies to memoir, and a possibility for both is to work with a framing device to explore your past. For example, the rationale for your outline could be an activity you are engaged in – a long walk, or trip, starting a garden, examining a painting – where different stages of that activity trigger memories, related one by one until you reach your destination or the 'framing' task is completed and you reflect upon and conclude your story.

Although some of your text will need corroborative information from other sources, most of your material is within your own memory and this can make planning more difficult than for other genres. Memories come haphazardly, we can often provoke them, but they are not amenable to the same kind of 'preliminary research' as other subjects. If you find that difficulty in creating a structure is blocking your progress, work initially directly from your timeline, writing memories as they surface in any order to record them while they are there. Once you accumulate a substantial amount of writing, look for patterns which might suggest both theme and structure and work from there.

In *Ammonites and Leaping Fish: A Life in Time* (Fig Tree), the 80-year-old novelist Penelope Lively relates her memoir in a three-part structure. Part one highlights images from her childhood memories; part two uses the volumes on her bookshelf as a frame for telling the stories of how she acquired them and what they mean to her; the final part applies the same device with her six most-treasured objects. Revealing a life story through possessions could work for many people; for others, actions might be more appropriate. It depends on the lives in question because structures must suit content and vice versa.

How-to and self-help:

Careful sequencing is essential in structuring a how-to book that describes the steps in achieving something. You may write: 'Now quickly place the paper that has already been soaked, onto the board.' What? If you didn't tell your reader to soak it at the appropriate time, she hasn't done it. She is stumped and she will hate you.

However, structure can be varied in other ways. At some point, a book on how to build your own house must have clear steps that begin with digging foundations and work upwards, with opening chapters on financing, land acquisition, design, surveying or planning consents, but variety can be achieved by interspersing sections with brief personal stories, or anecdotes about things going wrong.

For self-help books, I've already suggested starting with the benefits – the 'after' story – so that subsequent chapters can explore why and how changes were made. An alternative would be to structure the material around a series of personal case-studies, drawing conclusions from them and relating that to your theme. Polly Morland employs this method in *The Society of Timid Souls: Or, How to be Brave* (Profile Books). From a series of vignettes of individuals who faced horrific events with tremendous bravery – and not always surviving – she concludes that bravery is not a moral choice that we weigh up and make decisions about, but an instinct that drives us.

Educational and text books:

If your book is for an existing series or for an educational institution, the structure you can employ may be predetermined by the house style of the publisher. Where you wield a free hand, any of the above ideas could be applied to a wide variety of educational subjects. We've seen already a book on mathematics constructed of stories about each equation, and a history divided into chapters on particular kinds of people and their lives.

The attractiveness of a manual can be increased by organising the material around projects with specific examples, as in *Outdoor Classrooms: A Handbook for School Gardens* (Permanent Publications), by Carolyn Nuttall and Janet Millington. (This publisher specialises in environmental sustainability and has a special interest in 'permaculture'. A useful publisher to note if this is your area of expertise and you need to find a niche in this field or to source other books on these topics).

An entirely different approach is used by Sudhir Venkatesh in *Floating City* (Allen Lane). Venkatesh is a sociologist specialising in deep research: living alongside the people he investigates and sharing their lives (also called 'immersion research' or 'participative research'). *Floating City* contains material not included in academic papers normally issued after such projects because the contents are both personal and not measurable with the rigorous tools employed by academics – it was too anecdotal. But from a broader educational point of view, it opens a rich seam of material for understanding New York's 'under-life', and demonstrates the major challenge of participative research: remaining fully engaged while sustaining intellectual distance and perspective.

Venkatesh failed in this last respect, sharing with us his self-doubt and near breakdown through the experience. The result is a memoir, but the book is listed in the categories 'sociology' and 'economics', reflecting the depth of research and Venkatesh's stature both as an academic and an author in his subject. Bridging genres highlights new perspectives, but a publisher is more likely to accept the marketing risks of a split readership if a book is by an established author.

What about prefaces, introductions, prologues and epilogues?

Prologues are mainly used in fiction, but I once wrote a brief one as a playful piece to lighten the tone at the beginning of a nonfiction book of popular science. They should be used with caution. A prologue can tell a story as the backdrop to a book, but if the episode is so interesting that it's the first thing you want readers to see, it should be the opening hook of your first chapter. Nothing should go into a prologue that ought to be inside the book, and unless there is some exceptional reason why you need one, avoid it. Certainly don't plan for it at the start.

A preface is a brief statement by the author of the contents and scope of the book. It may also include his or her reasons for writing it or other background information – explanations that could equally go into an introduction if the book requires one for other purposes.

A foreword is an endorsement of the book and/or the author, usually written by an expert or celebrity figure in the genre. The value of this as a marketing feature is doubtful, but it can be effective in increasing an author's credibility. For example, in the case of a biography authorised by a member of the subject's family; or the owner of a historic building authenticating an account of its history.

Your book is likely to benefit from an introduction to prepare readers' expectations; 'how to use this book' advice; why you wrote it and where your expertise comes from, or some general background and context to the subject. Allow for it in your outline and, as you work through the book, note anything that comes to mind which is relevant, but it is better not to write an introduction until the manuscript is complete and the whole perspective is in your head.

One reason is that if the finished book is listed in online retail sites with 'Look Inside' features, it is the first impression of the book that a potential buyer receives. An introduction must be written with great care. Although it serves a useful purpose for readers, it inevitably becomes part of your promotion and marketing in the same way as the title and cover, and is best left till the end, when you know precisely what the book contains and your writing skills are at their peak.

Epilogues are even rarer than prologues and nearly always superfluous, containing material that should be woven into the final chapters. Or else they are extraneous 'pets' of the author's that don't need to be there at all. One example where readers might appreciate it is in an account of experiences that ended some years ago, and included details of people crucial to the event. If you know what has happened to some of those people since, but the information is not an appropriate way to conclude your final chapter, those personal updates could form an epilogue. But don't plan for an epilogue in your outline: wait to see if you need one.

Filling out your chapter outline:

If you are uncertain about where to put some of the sections you want to write about, don't spend too much time agonising over it: you have yet to complete deeper research which may produce new ideas and require updates to both the timeline and outline. And during the first full edit, it is easy enough to switch the order of one or two passages or chapters, if necessary.

What you are constructing is an initial guide: a draft outline to guide research. It is tentative at this stage and will be built up gradually as you move back and forth between research and structuring with your timeline and outline. The two processes run alongside each other in the early stages, but we start by organising our thoughts and existing material into a provisional structure – a work in progress that will be fine-tuned after you complete the bulk of your research.

Although it is important to think it through as carefully as you can at the beginning, everything can be tweaked at review and editing stage because, by then, your comprehensive timeline and refined chapter outline act as reference points.

Once you decide on the number of chapters and what to include in each, give a descriptive heading to each chapter (the fun of creating catchy chapter titles comes later), and you are ready to write a brief précis – a couple of sentences – on the key contents of each chapter, and why they are placed in that order. These form your initial chapter outline.

Finally, give your book a working title. 'Working' because choosing titles, like covers, is primarily a marketing decision and publishers generate their own ideas, and anyway, you may think of something better when you get to the end, but it is a good feeling to put a name to your book. It will be sharing your life for some time.

What to do now:

→ Compile your timeline. Check it carefully. Save as a separate document and print.

→ Determine the theme of your book and write that down alongside your purpose, readers and genre on the slip of paper that will remain pinned to the wall: your theme is part of how you make *your* book unique.

→ Using the timeline for reference, and bearing in mind your theme, construct your initial chapter outline and précis. Save and print.

You will then be ready for the final part of your plan: setting up your working space, equipment, resources and filing systems before you become overwhelmed by documents and folders. We cover that in the next chapter.

3

Create Your Set-up

You might think that, logically, this topic should have been covered at the start, but in my experience, the most important impetus to writers committing themselves to completing a book, is to know where they are going and to see something tangible on the table – their draft chapter outline – to motivate them before they deal with technical details and equipment for the long haul. So, when I worked on the structure for this book, I gave priority to reader motivation. My theme is the empowerment of another to compile a well-written nonfiction book: any author who wants her readers to write should lead their fingers to the keyboard as soon as possible. But now, we need some organisation.

Your Space:

Space is a problem for many writers, especially if they are part of a busy household. You need your own space, however modest, not only to keep references handy and protect your papers from becoming drawing fodder, but because a writing space is a mental anchor. Going to your own place attunes your mind to writing mode. It helps you to disregard all the other demands on your time and attention and to focus on your book.

If you can concentrate with distractions like X-Factor in the background (and a surprising number of people can), you might commandeer a corner of the lounge. If you're lucky, you have a spare bedroom, or a table with a shelf above in a laundry or utility room. Even a corner at the back of a garage would do.

In desperate circumstances, you could empty a couple of shelves in a storage cupboard and occupy the middle shelf as a surface for your laptop – it has the advantage that you can close the door to exclude adventurous little fingers in your absence. My first 'writing room' was a linen cupboard which proved to be a warm, comforting and inspiring place.

It is worth using your ingenuity to find a space for your writing; it will make a huge difference to your progress. But carry a notebook, too, for inspirational moments: ideas come anywhere at any time.

Your Time:

For most people, finding the time to write is even trickier than having their own space. Writers can become eccentric about their needs: "I *must* have complete silence and know there will be no interruptions for at *least* the next three days before I can write a *single word*!" If you wait for ideal conditions you will never write 'a single word' either.

If you haven't written much up to now, you have the advantage of being able to develop more realistic attitudes to where and when you write without such temperamental hang-ups. We are all trainable.

Ideally, you should write when your mind and energy are at their freshest – this might be early in the day for 'morning people'. For others, it might be when they feel 'free-est': after major demands on them have been met, and that is probably after everyone else has gone to bed. Work out which is the best time for you.

But the real key to both developing your writing skill and completing your book, is to write something – if only notes – every day, even for twenty minutes. The regularity creates continuity of learning and of thinking through what you are writing; it also encourages the brain to continue working on the project in the background, subconsciously, until your next writing session.

If you live with or share your life with others, writing your book will require a degree of collaboration: you may have to negotiate the time you need. Perhaps you can agree on a trade-off: certain uninterrupted times for you each day, in exchange for a period of your undivided attention to others in some special way. Or think of ways you could spark their imagination and cooperation by being involved, especially if your subject requires practical activities or visits to places. Oddly, these new arrangements could result in better 'quality contact' between you than existed before the pressure to find writing time.

Management of your time is an issue you should face and resolve at the outset, otherwise, guilt, hassle and resentment will sap your creative energy in vicious cycles.

Your computer and basic settings:

You will have realised by now that I assume you use a computer keyboard of some description. If you are not of the digital generation and view computers as adversaries, this is a war you must fight and win. Even if you feel more inspired when writing longhand, everything must be keyed-in at some point: even a manuscript intended only for private printing has to be on a computer file that a printer can access.

Unless you want to accept the errors, delays and costs, of others typing for you, you need to learn the basics of a computer writing programme: it is much quicker and easier to write, edit and correct than handwriting. Remember, we are all trainable.

Those of you who click your way around a PC with ease, can smile smugly and skim the following section, but don't skip it altogether, or you might miss a new trick.

The most commonly used computer programme among editors, publishers and everyone else in the industry is Microsoft Word: that is the file type they will expect for submitting a manuscript or proposal, and that is the programme I refer to in this section. The following is a list of basic actions for your set-up.

- If you have the choice of a desk-bound PC or a laptop, I recommend a laptop; its portability enables you to escape from unwanted visitors and the television, or to work in the local library and other locations.

- Acquire a spare hard drive (also called a 'zip drive') or a flash drive with sufficient capacity to hold all the files you will need for your project. If anything drastic happens to your computer, all your work should already be backed up on an external drive, either to re-install, or to access from another machine.

- After a working session, 'save', print new work (for added security and later editing), and back up by saving to the zip or flash drive. This is your mantra whenever you finish a writing session: save/print/back up. Machines fail or are stolen; files disappear (especially if you share a computer) and viruses kill software.

- For extra cover, arrange with a trusted friend to store copies of your critical files on his or her hard drive. Alternatively, you could use an online backup facility ('cloud storage') which is usually free.

- And if you don't possess a socket board with protection from power surges, this is the time to buy one.

- Create a document folder with the name of your book's working title, and save into it your statement of purpose, timeline and chapter outline files. Other files will go in later, but I make two other separate document folders: one for all research data as it is acquired; the other for the manuscript as I write it. No other files go into these two folders because it is easier for regularly backing up changes.

- A handy tip is to create a desktop short cut for these two folders so that you can open them quickly.

- Document files saved in Word bear the suffix .doc (or .docx in more recent versions). When sending files and unsure which version of Word your recipient uses, select the option under the 'Save As' menu to save in 'compatible mode'. You might occasionally be asked for a file in other formats such as Rich Text (.rtf) or PDF (.pdf) and these options are also in the dropdown menu of Save As.

- Check the default settings for 'auto-save' and set it to save at the most frequent intervals: you can write (and lose) a lot of precious words within 5 minutes. But get in the habit of saving your work as you go along by following a full stop with the 'save' action so that you don't even have to think about it.

- Choose the language setting for spell-check that is appropriate for you – nothing is more irritating if you're writing in British English than having spell-check unnecessarily underlining 'traveller' in censorial red, or worse, auto-correcting it to 'traveler'. I don't select auto-correct: for me, it causes more hassle than it avoids.

- Be aware that spell-check is not reliable for editing or proofreading: it will not, for example, tell you if you type 'bear' instead of 'bare' because both are correctly spelled words. A computer lacks the common sense to realise that you probably didn't mean you 'nuzzled a bear chest'.

- The first time you type an unusual personal or place name, or a foreign or technical word that spell-check doesn't recognise, it underlines it in red. Don't simply ignore this; check that you typed the word accurately, and enter it into spell-check's 'custom dictionary' – if you type it incorrectly later, spell-check will alert you.

- Choose your settings for grammar-check, but don't depend on it: it is not always right, but when you edit, those little green lines can alert you to a sentence that might be improved, or to an errant extra space between words.

- You could also turn on style-check at the beginning, just to keep you aware of how you are expressing yourself, but don't let it boss you around too much. It is all right, for example, to write sentence fragments on occasion. Really. And to start a sentence or paragraph with 'and' or 'but'.

Good working habits:

The final formatting of your document – alignment of text, spaces between lines and paragraphs, indents and margins – will depend on the manuscript's destination and requirements of an agent or publisher, but good working habits from the outset will save an enormous amount of hassle for you and others in the future.

Two important actions you should observe right from the start:

- Insert only one space after a full stop within a paragraph, and *no* space after a full stop at the end of a paragraph. If you insert more, every sinful extra space has to be hunted down and deleted by whoever is processing your manuscript for publication. And if that is you, tearing out your hair while trying to convert your Word document into digital format, well, I did warn you.

- Never create an indent, or adjust the width of an indent, by jumping up and down on the space bar, or backspace key. These, too, would need to be eliminated later. Use the tool bar, not the keyboard, for formatting. Indent by selecting the area of text and clicking the appropriate button in the 'paragraph' section of the tool bar along the top of your Word screen.

The usual final format required for nonfiction books is that there are no indented paragraphs (except for quotes or bullet points), and that text is double spaced and 'left' aligned for print, 'justified' for ebooks. But when I start writing, I select options from the tool bar to set up an interim working format that is comfortable and practical. Clicking the corner of the 'paragraph' section on the tool bar, I create the following settings:

- Space between paragraphs at 6 pt and line spacing at 1.5 because the text is clear and easy to read and to edit later, while not using too much paper when printing

- Text justified: simply my personal preference for the look of the screen

Using other parts of the tool bar –

- Font is set to Times New Roman 12pt, which is standard in the publishing industry

- Margins are set to 'normal'.

- Working in 'print layout' view, I adjust the zoom scale on the bottom right of the screen to 120% which provides a large enough text for easy reading, but still allows me to see half a page at a time.

- I insert 'page number' at the start, and so never have to waste time trying to collate printed pages when they fall off the desk and scatter on the floor.

You will spend a lot of time looking at the screen, so play around with the settings and discover what is comfortable for you.

Another convenient aid you can set up now is a hyperlinked Table of Contents (ToC) which you can update after each writing session with a single click, and which also enables you to access directly any chapter or subheading as your manuscript grows in length. In an ebook, the ToC is hyperlinked to the main text: clicking on any heading or sub-heading listed in the ToC, brings that piece of text onto the screen. For a print book, you will eventually need a Table of Contents, and while it can be typed and updated manually, it is a tedious and time-consuming exercise. Instead, you can set it up as a hyperlinked list from the start, using Word's automatic ToC tool, (you will find this by clicking on 'References' on the tool bar – 'Table of Contents' should appear on the left).

The ToC cannot be established until you have typed the title and chapter headings into your document and selected a style from the 'styles' section of the tool bar, but now you have the headings from your chapter outline, you can set up the ToC ready for when you start writing the manuscript. Open a new document and 'save as' in a new folder with the file name for your book, (this will be your main manuscript folder).

Type into the document your book's working title and, underneath, list the chapters and any subheadings you are using. The link below takes you to a Microsoft Word Tutorial which leads you through each step of selecting a style for your chapter headings and entering them into an automatic ToC. Note that if you decide later to select a different style, change the wording of chapter headings, or add subheadings, it is easy to do once the ToC is set up – you will not be 'stuck' with the words you choose now.

http://www.youtube.com/watch?v=9XkYZHKT_p8

(If you are using a different software version to that described in the tutorial, a search for 'Microsoft Word Table of Contents Tutorial' will bring up other options).

Once your ToC is established, click 'update entire table' after each writing session, and then 'save': it is essential to save after each update.

One other time saver from the tool bar that you should become familiar with: the 'Find' function (on the top right of the screen on my version of Word). Once your manuscript grows, it is irksome to scroll up and down looking for a particular word when you can't remember exactly where you wrote it. 'Find' will swiftly locate it for you. You can also find every instance of using a particular word – and be shocked at how you overuse it. But the 'replacement' facility is especially handy: if you realise, for example, that you've been writing 'Jeffrey' when it should be 'Geoffrey', 'replace all' can correct it throughout the document.

Before we leave the computer, it is worth considering a few ways of lessening its effects on our health.

Ensure the keyboard and reference documents being used are well lit; adjust the screen illumination to avoid glare; position the computer or laptop so that you can press the keys and see the screen with your back and neck straight, and position other materials where you can reach them, without lunging awkwardly sideways to a low drawer, for example.

An adjustable chair is ideal, especially one that supports the curve of your back. And it is important to move away from the computer at regular intervals to stretch, exercise and rest your eyes.

Many writers develop chronic back and neck pain. My own solution to this is to place the laptop on a custom-height stand on top of the desk, and to write while standing. It enables me to move my limbs freely at any time to maintain good circulation, and avoids back strain by spreading body weight evenly on both feet, rather than compressing the base of the spine. If you want to try this, start with short periods of standing and gradually prolong them. If you experience swollen ankles and feet at first, wear flight socks for a while until your body adjusts. I write standing, edit sitting; I think Hemingway did it the other way round.

Other resources:

Other resources you will need, if you don't own them already, are a good dictionary, and a thesaurus – preferably *Roget's Thesaurus*. Although the latter is described as a 'list of synonyms' – alternative words with the same meaning – no two words are exactly interchangeable and in that fact rests the real value of a thesaurus. It enables you to find a word that says *precisely* what you mean, instead of using, and possibly misusing or overusing, the word that comes quickest to your mind.

And it's worth looking around second-hand bookshops for other helpful references like specialist dictionaries, or books of quotations. A lot of information can be sourced on the Internet, but it is often quicker to pick up a book from your desk, and browsing through them can spark inspiration on days when your brain feels sluggish.

If you need other books or equipment for your subject, such as a recording device, camera or scanner; require access to specialist libraries; have to ask people if they are willing to be interviewed; or you want to practise a craft process you intend to write about, this is the time to make those arrangements so that lack of them does not delay you later.

People are resources, too, not only for information but for general support and encouragement. Writing a book can be lonesome. Think about joining a local writers' group, or an online forum. Be aware, though, when reading tips and advice, that most forums and writing blogs focus on writing fiction rather than nonfiction: the craft of putting sentences together may be the same, but the approach and planning process is not, as we've already seen. You might search a bit harder to find a nonfiction writers' site that suits you; some good places to start are listed in the Appendices under 'Useful Websites and Books'.

And perhaps there is someone you know who also writes or shares your particular interest, who might act as a sounding board or mentor, either by meeting occasionally or through email correspondence. A writing buddy can ease your journey.

What to do now:

→ Arrange your computer settings and create your first document folders and files.

→ If necessary, study a basic book on using Microsoft Word and identify someone locally who could be a technical guru if you find yourself in trouble.

→ Buy, borrow or beg the equipment and resources necessary for your project, and start a system for recording expenditure and keeping receipts: if you are liable to pay tax on earnings from your book, you will need these to claim expenses.

→ Look at your timeline and make any advance arrangements required for access to people, information or places, and set up a system for keeping track of correspondence and contact details. You will need these soon because our next stage is to begin research.

→ To test out your settings and begin developing the writing style for your book, write a 1,000-word piece about any topic from your timeline – whatever inspires you at this moment, whether or not it will feature in a chapter. Write it with your readers in mind: 'talk' to them. Leave it for a week before reviewing and editing until it is the best you can do at this stage. Save, print, and back up the document because this article will perform other tasks for you later.

→ Continue reading, not only books in your genre but quality newspapers to experience good nonfiction writing. *The Guardian Weekly*, for example, is a compilation of the best features from *The Observer*, *The Guardian*, *Le Monde* and *The Washington Post* and has world-wide coverage. You will read there some of the best-written journalism, and it is a good way to remain up to date in most fields.

4.

Gather Your Information

All writing is founded on research in some form. Even a self-help book based on an author's personal experience needs evidence to support the advice offered to readers; this is part of the writer's credibility. No one will believe a claim that they can lose 4kgs a week with little effort and no ill effects unless it really has been 'tried and tested' and checkable proof is presented.

You may already have accumulated a lot of data – for example, journals and photographs for a travelogue, albums and letters for a family history, or records of craft production – but your book is likely to include background information, technical explanations and comparisons which require research, and your existing data may need verification and updating.

Whatever the topic of your book, it is unlikely that you would be able to amass all the information at once and for most subjects it is not necessary. You might access the bulk of material at the beginning, but research is an on-going activity until the manuscript is complete: while writing, ideas may come to you that need validating and, when editing, you will notice things that should be checked and clarified.

The priority for your research plan is to tackle the material that is fundamental to your whole 'story': data that could influence your chapter outline, or even your chosen theme. This initial research will substantiate the plan and approach you mapped out earlier. Refer to your timeline to direct what you search, and as you work through it, update the timeline and chapter outline as necessary, or note that an area of the subject has now been checked. In this way, you progress with research and refine your chapter outline concurrently.

Subsequent research should continue to be carried out with one eye on the chapter outline to remind yourself what you need to know and how you will apply it. Finding a new and exciting study of a favourite subject is seductive; it will eat up all your time unless you ask yourself: How is this relevant? How would I use it? Do I really need it for this book?

Researching for a book follows what is called an 'iterative' process – going back and forth repeatedly between sources of information and the plan that guides where you are going and determines how the data is applied. However, before you start, you need to know about various sources and methods of research and the reliability of the facts they produce.

Types of data:

It is important to recognise the difference between 'quantitative' data and 'qualitative' data because you are likely to be using the results of both in one way or another.

Quantitative data – from the word 'quantity' – uses numbers to describe things that can be measured or counted. It might be production figures; the percentage of households who work more than eight hours a week in their gardens; the population of a town; the number of children suffering from obesity; the age of an antiquity; or the length of a bumble-bee's tongue (yes, someone has measured that, too, and it can be as long as 12mm).

In assessing the reliability of quantified data, look first at the credentials of the researcher or the institution that carried it out, and whether they might have a vested interest in the results (who funded the work for example). Then check the definitions used (what is meant by 'obese'), and the size or location of the sample (the number of people who answered the questions) – if the gardening survey was carried out on only 100 people in a rural area, then the data should not be applied generally to a whole region that includes cities, because fewer urban residents own gardens.

Often, it is not the research that is at fault, but the way writers apply it and describe it. Any statement quoting numbers can seem persuasive on first reading: '70% of the sample that ate a serving of spinach at least three times a week showed higher scores for intelligence.'

Before we all rush off to eat spinach: Higher than what? – Their cat? Their own scores *before* eating spinach? The 30% who didn't eat spinach? Such examples are not hard to find.

For historical studies, making 'then and now' comparisons has its own hazards: if both sets of data were not gathered and calculated in the same way, the reliability of conclusions as to what has changed over a given period is limited.

Even the statistical formulae may be questioned: some are more appropriate for certain subjects, and small samples require special procedures.

Because of this, most quantitative results are quoted with an estimate of 'degrees of error'. Experts in a subject know how to assess relevant data; lay-people should quote others' research results with informed caution, but we will see, later, a way of gauging the reliability of the 'facts' we find.

Qualitative data – not so simply related to 'quality' because both quantitative and qualitative data can be of high or low quality – refers to information which cannot be measured with certainty, or perhaps not at all, but nevertheless may supplement and enrich quantitative results, or be tapped as the main data source in some types of research.

Sociologists, social anthropologists, historians and journalists all make extensive use of qualitative data to gather peoples' opinions, feelings, behaviours and explanations of events in their lives and the lives of those around them. But we must be careful about interpreting information when the questions are put to people with a different culture, or whose mother tongue is another language, because they may not be answering the question we think we are asking.

Surveys, interviews, focused discussion groups or informally guided conversations are all valuable ways of gathering information for a range of topics, including local history, memoir, travel and current issues. Such personal and anecdotal information can add depth, local colour and emotional engagement to nonfiction writing; quoting people directly lets the reader 'hear' their voices and relate to them. The problems arise when this data is quoted to 'prove' an idea; is passed off as 'fact', or is applied beyond its context as a general 'truth'.

Sources of information:

Misinformation in both forms of data is abundant online and in print. The saying: 'Believe none of what you hear and only half of what you read,' contains much wisdom, but fortunately, there are ways of gauging the reliability of information we discover during research. The most important method is to reference more than one source, so you can compare them. Professional researchers use the term 'triangulation': if three different sources agree, the data are likely to be correct. But we need to go one step further.

A problem with global information and the speed and ease of dissemination is that the same information − or misinformation − is repeated in many places: what you think are different sources, turn out to be the same source 'shared' and leaked all over the Internet. The solution is to explore several media and include at least one primary source in your triangle.

A primary source is the original information as it was first discovered or observed, whether quantitative or qualitative: accounts of travellers past and present; the results of field research by anthropologists or archaeologists, and the discoveries of scientists, for example. Primary sources include direct observations recorded by someone with credibility in that area or topic, and other original documents, such as correspondence or official papers, diaries, and family albums. If you are writing about authors, artists, or musicians, study their original works rather than depend on someone else's review or crib-notes.

For writers of memoir or biography, birth, death and marriage certificates, school reports, correspondence and a last will and testament are all significant primary sources.

Secondary sources rework extracts from primary data for further discussion, or to relate it to other topics. Secondary sources are more readily available and can offer valuable insight and synthesis, especially for the tuning-in stage of your research; they can also provide links to primary sources and other reading in their bibliographies. An indication of reliability for secondary data is whether it cites its primary sources sufficiently for you to check them out if you wish.

Books and articles are sources of both primary and secondary data. Make friends with your local library – it will stock a range of valuable reference books. And although you are writing nonfiction, relevant novels, films and magazines can give you a general feel for a place or period and excite your own creativity; so can pictures and music. Photographs, both old and recent are a further significant source of information, especially if details of the subject and date are recorded.

Although searching the Internet should be carried out with a critical eye, search engines can identify reliable information – including primary data – especially for places and environments (Google Earth), and on the websites of universities, libraries, or specialist institutions, many of which give access to original documents. (You may be required to register and/or pay for these). Make full use of freely available material that is no longer subject to copyright and therefore part of 'the commons'; sites like Project Gutenberg and The Public Domain Review are excellent for history, literature and art. (Web addresses to these and other relevant sites are given in the Appendices).

Wikipedia is better moderated than when it was first established, but never depend upon it as your only source, especially if no references are listed; if they are, some of these might lead you to primary and secondary sources.

From site visits or field research you create your own primary data. You can also gather information by taking part in social situations – called 'participant observation'. What you witness must be recorded accurately during the observations or as soon afterwards as possible, while it is still clear in your mind, especially if you want to note dialogue. A recording device and camera are excellent ways of 'fixing' what you see and hear 'on location'; you can add analysis, comparisons and other thoughts to your journal later.

Depending on the topic of your book, field research can help you establish the atmosphere of historic sites; experience travel locations; appreciate places where the subjects of biographies or memoirs once lived; understand social, industrial or administrative processes, or enable you to witness events. And for practical books – on traditional crafts, or gardening, for example – field trips to other enthusiasts enable you to compare methods and applications, producing not only information but also interesting pictures and quotations.

If you are not a scientist, you may think that experimental or laboratory research – another important source of primary data – does not apply to you. But if you write a practical how-to book on topics such as cooking, model making, herbal remedies or building, for example, your 'laboratory' is your own kitchen or backyard. However familiar you are with your subject, when describing steps and processes for others to follow, it is advisable to test out the methods, take careful notes and photographs of each stage, and identify and resolve possible snags. Readers expect advice on what to do when things go wrong.

Using photography as research:

The information you gather from both field trips and practical research should include photographs. Images are visual field notes and sources of information for you, but also add interest to your book. Illustrations are expected in books these days, especially as modern technology removes any cost penalty to the number of high quality images you can insert into a digital book. Many photographs are available free on the Internet, but in most cases, the better quality pictures needed for publication, especially for print, are copyright and paying for licence to use them becomes expensive. It is better to take your own pictures, if possible.

Sourcing images from elsewhere may be necessary for historical research, from museums, for example, and you will be asked to pay for these, but for books about a product – e.g. vintage cars, chocolate, toys or clothing – manufacturers might be pleased to provide you with illustrations. Be careful about scanning pictures from old books: the book itself may be out of copyright but the images may not be.

For making your own illustrations you will need high resolution photographs, and although the technology is developing rapidly, snaps taken with a cell phone are unlikely to be good enough quality for publishing in print, or even in an ebook. They might look all right as small images on a website, but when enlarged, low resolution pictures break up into overlapping patches of colour (pixelation) that completely distort the subject.

Digital image files are stored and emailed, or posted on a web page, in a reduced form called 'jpeg' files (usually 640 x 480 pixels) to save space, but for publication, the original resolution of an image when taken by the camera should be at least 2272 x 1704 pixels. To take photographs like these you need access to a digital camera with a specification of around 12 megapixels and with the camera's menu set to 'superfine'. High resolution shots take up a lot of memory space, so buy high capacity memory cards (at least 1GB) and always carry spares.

Compact cameras with in-built lenses are small enough to slip into your pocket, but if high quality photography is important to your book, you will probably already know that a digital SLR (single-lens reflex) camera, which has interchangeable lenses, allows far greater creative and technical freedom.

Expensive, highly sophisticated photo-editing software is not essential (unless photography is your passion). Picasa® (a Google product) will allow you to carry out as much editing and enhancing as you are likely to require and is free to download. If you need help using digital photography, I recommend Gavin Hoole and Cheryl Smith's book: *Really, Really, Really Easy Step-by-Step Digital Photography* published by New Holland. It is based on Picasa® software and covers taking, storing, editing and using your pictures in various creative ways, (and is a good example of a how-to book on a technical subject).

Set up a proper filing system for your images from the start: you will want to know who or what is in an image long after you took it, and to locate it among hundreds of others on your hard drive. All your photo-files should also be saved on your spare hard drive and with an online backup service if you use one.

Data from interviews:

The other principle means to create your own primary data is through interviews; especially for gathering the memories of local 'worthies' and older people for local histories, and the stories and reminiscences of friends and family members for memoirs. And for travelogues, you can arrange interviews or make notes on informal 'guided conversations' with local inhabitants, other travellers, or tourism providers. Personal anecdotes, views and memories help to create a fuller picture of a location and provide a deeper human dimension.

When interviews reveal information that you want to quote as fact rather than opinion, you should verify it through other sources. But personal views and histories are valuable in their own right, especially if you want to show the fullest possible character of a person who is featured in your book.

On whatever subject you write, including the perspectives and quotes of other people will make your account more vivid and enable readers to feel emotionally engaged. Pure desk research can become a dry read, detached from human concerns. At the very least, interviewing others will allow you to share their enthusiasm and commitment; stimulation that will show in your writing.

Interviewing is a skill in its own right – asking questions in the wrong way can skew the answers, or result in no answer at all – but it is an essential ability for nonfiction writers, so here are tips on how to make each interview successful.

How to Create a Successful Interview:

Prepare beforehand:

- Check your chapter outline to decide exactly what information you hope to gather, and identify the best person to provide it: someone who has the relevant experience and knowledge, or is at the right level of an organisation to tell you what you want to know. If your interest is daily activities in a hospital ward, ask nurses and patients, not the Director of the Health Trust.

- There may be value in interviewing couples or small groups, but hold follow-up interviews with individuals if you can, because people may curb their expression in the presence of others.

- Interviewees will expect to be told why you want to talk with them. Obviously, you want to engage their cooperation, but unless you seek specific facts, indicate your general area of interest rather than exactly what you hope to find out, otherwise it might limit their responses and you could miss gems you didn't realise you needed to know.

- Make arrangements in advance that are convenient for the interviewee; (arrive on time and leave when you said you would).

- Do your homework: don't waste time by asking for personal or other information that is readily available elsewhere, unless you need to double-check the facts, if so, say you are doing this.

- Test the recording device if you intend to use one. Check that you have notebook and backup pens and, if you made one as a personal reminder, the list of issues you want to cover.

- Depending on who you will interview and why, consider whether to record their responses for later transcription, to take notes as they talk, or to memorise as much as possible and write it down immediately afterwards. Modern recording devices are unobtrusive; most cell phones will record, but it may be alien to an elderly person, for example – ask if they mind being recorded before you switch it on. Some people clam-up in the presence of recorders and you may prefer to take discreet notes, rather than come away with no interview at all.

- If you want some information verbatim, you need to write notes on those responses, but allow time to just sit and listen as well. Sometimes people are distracted by interviewers taking notes. And if you are scribbling constantly, you can't listen deeply, notice body language, or maintain eye contact.

During the interview:

- Whether you are interviewing your grandmother, a fellow

professional or a complete stranger of senior or junior status, style your dress, greeting, and initial 'warm-up' to suit the situation.

- Chat informally for a few minutes to establish a relationship and to put the interviewee at ease. If you sit back in your chair and look relaxed – the interviewee is more likely to do the same.

- If it seems appropriate, offer, or accept, refreshments. Food is best avoided, it takes up time to eat, and neither of you can talk with a mouth full of double-chocolate muffin.

- Start with simpler questions closer to home: "How did you get involved in running a restaurant?" Rather than: "How are global trade agreements affecting your food imports?"

- Know the difference between closed questions (used for facts or yes/no answers) and open questions (which encourage free-ranging responses), and apply them appropriately. For example: "Did you have to walk far to attend school?" (Closed question). The response is likely to be: "No, not really." Or: "About two miles." But if you want their experience and feelings about attending school, ask: "What was it like, attending school in those days?" (Open question). The interviewee will answer more fully with issues that are most important to him or her.

- Ask probing questions to extend the responses, or to home-in on a point you are especially interested in: "What happened then?" "How did it feel when that happened to you?" "What else did the boss say to you?" "Could you give me an example?" But speak in a relaxed, conversational tone: it is not an interrogation.

- Ask clarifying questions for important points that are not clear to you, and signal what you are doing: "Going back to when you first arrived in the country, did you say only your mother came with you? Was it just the two of you who emigrated?" And: "I don't quite understand how you lost your house after the war, can you tell me more about that?"

- Subtly guide the interview in the direction you want it to go, but don't keep interrupting to impose your own sequence of ideas – to learn what people have to say it is better to let them follow their own logic; it's your job to sort out the results later.

- Do not 'lead the witness': in general, interviewees try to be helpful, if you put ideas into their heads: "There wouldn't have been many visitors around then, would there?" – You will simply get your own ideas quoted back to you.

- Avoid *telling* people what they feel; that's what you are trying to find out. If you say: "That must have been very frustrating, or very sad, for you." – She may agree with you whether it was really significant for her or not. Instead, ask: "How did you feel about it?" "Would you do it all again?"

- Encourage responses and show empathy with occasional nods and smiles, and non-committal expressions such as: "I see." "I can understand that." "Hmm, it must have been." "Why was that?" "That's interesting, can you tell me a bit more about it?"

- If the interviewee draws you into discussion, you should respond in a friendly manner, but keep it brief and steer the conversation back to the interviewee and the subject as tactfully and quickly as you can. Don't be diverted into spending precious contact time on your own stories or opinions.

- Most people enjoy talking about themselves and their interests to a sympathetic listener. Once you get the interview going, apart from adding specific questions, or a little tactful steering occasionally, you should be listening carefully most of the time rather than talking.

- Give some signals that the interview is coming to a close with phrases such as: "May I ask you one last question?" Or: "What advice would you give to others after your experience?" "What did you learn from what you went through?" And: "Is there anything else we haven't talked about?" Sometimes, this question opens up the seam of a gold mine.

- Wind down with friendly chat. Arrange to borrow photographs or other documents, or set a further interview if necessary, and be sure to thank them for their time and interest.

Those are the key points for carrying out a good interview on a wide range of topics, but there are some special situations. If you are writing a biography and your subject, or someone close to them if they are no longer living, has agreed to help you with your book, you will be establishing a longer-term relationship; the initial interview will be the first of a series, so don't rush to get all the answers at once. For this sort of research, you need to build mutual trust because you want a deep understanding of your subject – their experiences, personality and emotions. The same will apply to key interviewees for compiling local histories, memoirs and autobiographies.

A different situation altogether could arise if your book examines some topical issue involving errors or failings by companies and institutions resulting, for example, in environmental damage or political corruption. If you have a resistant interviewee, your approach will be more direct and persevering, but it is a balancing act: too much pressure could result in the interviewee simply walking out.

For this kind of interview, double-check the background information before you start and ensure your questions are specific and not ambiguous; insist on recording the interview (unless information is given 'off the record', in which case it is of limited value), and confirm critical answers: "Did you say the minister approved that in writing?" "No safety regulations were in force at the time, did I get that right?" And when you write the manuscript, be meticulous about accuracy of quotes and attributing facts and opinions: reluctant interviewees may attempt to discredit you if they don't like what you have published.

The material you gather from interviews can be used in several ways:

- To provide you with general background and inspiration for beginning your project, during which you might even find a potential mentor or collaborator.

- To inform you about ideas, places or people you should put into your chapter outline and research further.

- To enrich your book with direct quotations, atmosphere, and a human dimension.

- To reconstruct an event, past or present. For this, tap additional sources for corroboration – newspaper reports, official documents – and interview several people to compare their accounts. If you find no 'agreed' description you can employ as facts, writing about the different versions people experienced and remembered, and why that might be so, could also make an interesting chapter to your book – an example of adjusting your plan to the results of your research.

Finally, keep all your recordings, images and notes somewhere safe. There are important reasons for retaining accurate and detailed records of all your research and we cover this topic next.

Keep track of your information and stay out of trouble:

From the outset, keep detailed records of your searches, and sources of primary and secondary data:

- You will need the information to cite sources you quote and to construct your bibliography.
- You will be able to find them again when you want to check something or gather further information.
- If what you write is challenged for accuracy, or for libel, your records will be required as evidence.

Referencing your sources:

For books, magazines and other documents, a simple card index is useful for noting the title, author, publisher, and date and place of publication, and for making a few notes on the contents. Always record the page number for anything you might wish to quote verbatim. If materials are only on loan to you, it's better to take too many notes rather than too few, in case you can't access a source again. As you accumulate your own physical documents, set up a system of filing or shelving them for easy retrieval – I use flat-pack cardboard box files and label them clearly on the outside.

If possible, scan key documents to make copies, and store them directly into a computer file where they can be saved and backed up.

You can also open a new computer document file for 'Sources and References' and begin listing them for your bibliography. If you enter them gradually from the beginning in alphabetical order of authors' names, it avoids the Herculean task of dealing with them all at the end. A properly constructed bibliography will impress potential publishers. A standard layout, punctuation and formatting for listing references – called the Harvard System – is given below (use of capitals for the family name is optional).

For listing books –

NEVILLE, C. (2010) *The Complete Guide to Referencing and Avoiding Plagiarism*. Second Edition. Maidenhead: Open University Press.

If there is more than one author, list all of them in the same way before the year of publication. If the book is a collection of material by several authors brought together by an editor, list the editor:

WRIGHT, S. (ed.) (1994) *Anthropology of Organisations*. London and New York: Routledge.

To list a chapter from a collection, start with author and chapter title (note that only the book title, not the chapter title, is italicised).

NICHOLSON, T (1994) Institution Building: Examining the fit between bureaucracies and indigenous systems. In Wright, S. (ed.) *Anthropology of Organisations*. London and New York: Routledge.

For articles in journals, newspapers and magazines, begin with author and title (noting that only the publication is italicised) and quote volume and page numbers:

GREENE, M. C. and DONAHUE, J. K. (2011) Persistence of belief change in the face of deception: The effects of factual stories revealed to be false. *Media Psychology*. 14 (3). pp. 312-331.

BARON-COHEN, S. (2011) Evil is in reality a lack of empathy. *The Weekly Guardian*. 8th April. p.32.

For online references, start with author and title as above, putting the name of the website or publication in italics followed by [online]. State the date, and any page or section reference, followed by the URL, and quote in square brackets the date you accessed the article or post.

When writing more formally, for text books or educational books for example, if you quote from one of these sources or cite them as an authority, you simply put the author's last name and year of publication in brackets within the text – (Neville 2010) – so that readers can locate it in the bibliography.

It is a good idea to 'Bookmark' or 'Favourite' web pages that you want to quote, or might want to refer to again later, to avoid the time-wasting frustration of trying to locate a critical article you saw on the web last week that now seems to be hiding behind several million other websites. Print anything absolutely essential: websites can 'crash' or disappear, and internet connections fail at the time you want to access something.

Plagiarism and copyright:

Reading around your subject and finding relevant sources of information is essential but you must avoid plagiarising others' work. If you copy what someone else has written – even if you change a few words here and there – and pass it off as your own work, it is plagiarism. Others will notice and this little 'short-cut' will cost you your reputation, and possibly land you in legal difficulties. If drawing on another writer's work as a source of ideas or data, you must either quote brief passages verbatim, citing the author (see 'copyright' below), or rework the information entirely in your own words.

When jotting down extracts from sources, make it clear in your notes whether this is a quote or is written in your own words: you might forget later, and inadvertently plagiarise the author – I put a large 'Q' beside any notes that are copied directly from a source.

All those who create original text and images – including writers, artists, musicians, inventors of digital games and designers of websites – own the exclusive right to use their creations, and to gain financial benefit from their work by selling it or agreeing to its use or publication by others: this is their copyright. As an author, it will be your copyright, too.

Some content and images, especially on the Internet, are specified as being part of 'the commons' – freely available for downloading and quoting without breaching anyone's copyright. In any other circumstance, to use an image, or quote from someone else's work – even if you credit them as the originator – is breach of their copyright and could land you in costly court proceedings unless you get written permission from the copyright holder. Even after an author dies, someone – usually their publisher – holds and protects the copyright on their behalf as part of managing their literary estate.

Permission could involve a fee and is something you would have to budget for if you decide it is essential to include a particular passage in your book. Copyright conditions vary in different countries and are changing along with everything else in publishing: always seek permission rather than make assumptions.

In practice there are a couple of exceptions to the above that are useful to know:

- If it is more than 70 years since an author's death, their copyright lapses and their work becomes freely available to quote (provided you cite the author).

- It is considered 'fair use' to quote a brief passage (up to five lines, for example) without seeking permission, especially for educational purposes – again, the author must be credited. Oddly, this does not apply to songs, and permission to quote even a single line from a song is rarely granted.

Although there is no copyright on ideas and facts, there is on the research that produced them and the creations that result from them. You may think of the same idea as another, but where it came from and what you do with it must be your own original work. Titles and names are not covered by copyright, either, but they, along with words and phrases, can be registered by a company as a trademark which provides similar protection to prevent them being freely copied by others.

Most publishers display a 'permissions' page on their websites. Check them to see their policy on quotations and the procedure for obtaining their permission.

Libel and liability:

Libel is a complex and treacherous field of law. Basically, you libel or defame someone if you publish any statement that could demean them in the eyes of others, lead to their being socially excluded or ridiculed, or adversely affect their esteem in their place of work. They are not required to prove these affects have happened to them: the potential is sufficient to make a libel claim which the court decides.

It is a particularly sensitive area for writers of biography and memoir when you might be revealing intimate details of people's lives. 'Not meaning to cause harm' is no defence; neither is being suggestive without quoting a name if the court deems others could identify the person described. That the statement may be true is a slippery plea because of the difficulties of providing absolute proof sufficient to satisfy the court.

And don't think you'll be safe to include in your travelogue a fascinating tale of wicked deeds told to you in the wilds of some remote corner of the world. Biologist and author Jared Diamond published in the *New Yorker* a story of tribal payback killings that he heard about on a field trip in Papua New Guinea, and was pursued with a $10million suit for libel.

A business or corporation can claim it has been libelled, and so can family members of a deceased person if they feel themselves disparaged by your comments about their relative. In a book about literature, music, or film, for example, you could write a scathing review of an author's or actor's performance, but not about them personally. Critique the work, not the person.

Publishers dislike having to hire libel lawyers to check doubtful manuscripts, and being involved in a libel suit, even if it fails, will damage your own reputation. Be extremely cautious in what you write about people, and keep all your notes and recordings.

Liability is also a tricky legal area. If readers follow practical advice you offer and things go wrong – they lose money, are injured, become ill and so on – they may attempt to blame you for the instructions you gave them. In such cases, much depends on how accurately your advice was followed, but it is better to avoid being embroiled in the first place. Apart from checking scrupulously what you write, you should include clear references to health and safety practices and to stages when inexperienced readers should seek expert help. If you included none of these cautions, a disclaimer of liability in the front of your book may not carry much weight.

This issue is particularly important for books giving recommendations on health issues, physical or psychological. Be careful about the claims you make and the evidence you cite. Even if you are medically qualified, it should be made clear in several places in your book, that you are offering general guidance which should not be applied as individual diagnosis and treatment, and that readers with health problems should consult a health practitioner.

What to do now:

→   Set up files and systems for storing your data.

→   Begin the initial research which will validate your timeline and the draft chapter outline, updating both as necessary. Start with whatever data is accessible, you may have to wait for some information, from interviews or field trips for example, but you can feed-in this material as it becomes available.

→ As you progress, take breaks from research to develop the initial précis of each chapter into 300-word summaries. Write in proper sentences rather than notes or lists, because this will help you to develop a concise, clear style. Stay as close as you can to the word count: it will help you pick priorities – you are looking for the major elements only, the ones that reflect your theme and influence other items that there won't be room to mention specifically in the précis.

→ Alternate research with working on chapter summaries until your chapter outline is complete. Leave it for a few days, then edit and revise until you feel it gives the core of each chapter clearly enough to guide your writing.

You may need other details later, when you approach the full write up of each chapter, but once your chapter outline is complete, you are ready to start writing the first draft of your manuscript, which we talk about next. It won't matter which chapter you start with – it could be the easiest, the one for which there is most data, or your favourite aspect – because your plan keeps you on the right route.

The research and chapter outline can take almost as much time to work through as the actual writing because they are the foundation of your book: they determine the quality of what you write.

Part Two

Get it Down

5.

Write Your First Draft:

The second part of this chapter provides specific guidance for writing in different genres, but this first part offers essential advice, whatever the subject of your book, and we start with 'style'.

Creative writing for nonfiction:

Writing style:

Style is about how we express ourselves in any form. How we talk, dress, write – the animation of our personality. But we are complex beings and present ourselves in various ways in different situations. We dress suitably for each function, and we talk and write using appropriate words according to the circumstances and the people we are addressing. Yet there is a thread of consistency running through the ways we declare ourselves and what we stand for, which is a reflection of our values and character.

It follows that our style influences what we write about, as well as how we write it – our choice of images, phrasing, sentence construction, and how we address the reader. These are all elements of the 'writer's voice'. But in the same way that we adjust our clothing to the situation, we can adapt our 'voice' to suit the subject, purpose and audience of our writing.

Those who write a lot develop a style that is recognisably theirs, and may be known for more than one style. There is no right or wrong style, in the same way that there is no right or wrong personality, but the style should fit the subject and theme: they work together. Rather than trying to classify different writing styles, it may help in identifying an appropriate approach for your book if we look at two distinctive styles. We can then see how to apply elements of both for different purposes.

A didactic style is one that teaches, tells, and instructs from a position of authority, or at least, with confidence in its expertise. It is sometimes interpreted as 'talking down' to people although that depends on how it is used. A didactic approach is largely theoretical: applied to a college course, it means the teaching is based on reading text books rather than students' guided practice and discovery.

Writers using a didactic style are likely to include statistics and other quantitative data more than qualitative and descriptive information, and base their work on strict logic. In Europe, didacticism was the principal form of writing in the 19th century, and as a result, has a bad reputation for excessive moralising and distancing itself from readers who were expected to 'read, mark, learn and inwardly digest' for self-improvement. Today, it is applied more in academic writing than in 'popular' nonfiction, but its serious intent and anchoring in evidence has a broader role that we can employ, depending on our subject.

A narrative style is based on storytelling: the presence of characters to enact events which create causes and effects; the use of imaginative description, and the exploration of relationships between things – all woven together to send a message which readers can relate to emotionally. Storytelling can also convey facts; the narrative may not be 'invented' at all, but it draws upon qualitative information to provide meaning which can deeply affect a reader and their subsequent attitudes and behaviour. The reader is beguiled into understanding, rather than bombarded with information.

Storytelling is the oldest form of expression, going back to prehistoric oral traditions. It played a significant role in our evolutionary history, resulting in our brains being structured to understand everything as a narrative – it is how our minds work, the way we think and how we learn.

Clearly, logical sequencing, precise data, clear instructions and confidence in the knowledge being shared, are essential in a text book or a practical how-to book. Without them, students will not learn their history, sponge cakes will not rise and small businesses never prosper.

And yet, we understand and learn best through the emotional engagement and empathy created by storytelling. How do we resolve this dilemma?

Not only instructional and educational books, but all nonfiction is based on verifiable facts. However, we can employ elements of narrative style – creative writing techniques – to engage readers without inventing characters that did not exist, or events which never took place. This style is called 'narrative nonfiction'.

The term used primarily in the USA – 'creative nonfiction'– has a slightly different emphasis in that this form of writing usually puts the author at the centre of the work; a subject is examined through the experience of the author as narrator. This is not appropriate for all subjects, so I use the term 'narrative nonfiction' to mean applying a narrative style in various ways, even in text books. I suggest ideas to achieve this for different genres later in this chapter, but first, a few more general considerations.

Narrators and points of view:

A formal didactic style avoids close personal pronouns – 'I' and 'you'. Instead, the author refers to himself indirectly: 'the author spent five years', or 'this writer does not concur'. You are simply 'the reader' if he refers to you at all, which is one reason why this style is so distancing. There is no narrator as such, only the author.

In the narrative style, there is a narrator who reveals what the author wants to tell us and who may or may not be the author herself.

Who you decide upon to narrate your book – the storyteller/teacher – is related to the point of view, or perspective, from which the book will be written. There are no strict rules about which point of view to select, but each has specific possibilities and limitations which will determine which is most appropriate for your subject. In this book, I am the narrator sharing my knowledge, and I make use of all three principal points of view in different places for different reasons.

'First person' point of view –

In a 'first person' point of view, the writer is describing her own experience, thoughts or feelings, and uses 'I/my'. When I wrote: 'I find this helpful to forward-plan my research' I wrote in the first person: it describes my own method, which no one else could know about until I mentioned it.

When I used 'we/our': 'We can employ elements of narrative style' I included you, the reader, in a first person perspective because the statement applies to all of us writing nonfiction. The 'we', if used appropriately, draws the reader in to participate in what the writer is doing, but can become irritating if over-used or used incorrectly. For example, a nurse, who is clearly not on her lunch break, saying to a patient: "We are going to eat our nice lunch now." Or worse: "We woke up a little grumpy this morning, didn't we?" The irritation occurs because no one can know the true state of another's inner feelings unless they choose to tell us.

'Second person' point of view –

In a 'second person' point of view, a writer uses 'you/your'. When I wrote: 'Even if you intend your book to be shared only with family and friends, you will still want that written heritage to be the best you can write', I was making an *assumption* about you because I can't *know* what your attitude towards your writing really is (but I hope my assumption is right). Authors write in second person in this way to enlist a reader's feelings; it encourages reflection as to whether or not the assumption is correct, and it sets out an author's expectation of the reader.

More often, second person is employed when giving instructions or advice – it addresses readers directly and brings them closer to the author than alternative phrases such as 'one should', 'readers should' or 'the operative should'. However, point of view can be varied; other parts of a how-to book can be written in the first person, or even third person depending on the purpose of a particular chapter.

'Third person' point of view –

A 'third person' point of view describes the actions of other individuals, but in nonfiction, it cannot include their intentions or desires because they are inside a person's head and inaccessible to an observer. When I wrote: 'Biologist and author Jared Diamond published in the *New Yorker* a story of payback killings' I used a third person perspective. I was not there to observe him, but I know what he did because I accessed written evidence; what I can't know is what he thought or felt about it, or what his motives were, unless he explains them himself.

A third person perspective is commonly found in biographies, histories, and documentaries about prominent people or current issues. Although people featured in them 'come alive' to readers when they are described with the sort of detail novelists apply to their characters, a nonfiction author must not impute people's thoughts and feelings without clear evidence, such as diaries, journals, letters and interview transcripts. What appears to an onlooker to be an act of anger may be no such thing. What others say about a person is 'hearsay' and should be identified as such when used.

With a third person perspective, the narrator is normally the author 'talking' about people and events, and may add his or her own comments in a first person voice. To write in the 'second person' – to address readers directly – in a biography for example, would be unusual and possibly distracting for a reader.

Memoirs, autobiographies and travelogues are usually written in the first person voice of the author – who is then the only possible narrator – because the main purpose of these genres is to relate a unique, personal experience. Strangely, Salman Rushdie wrote his autobiography in the third person, which meant writing about his thoughts and feelings as if they were someone else's – as a novelist would – and I would love to know what was in his mind when he made that decision.

A family history could be told from the third person perspective of any one member of the family with the author as narrator – provided there is sufficient written or verbal information from that person to tell the family's story, or a significant part of it.

There are no rules, only guidelines, because choice of viewpoint depends on what gives the author the best route to exploring a particular subject and, as we shall see, there are various possibilities for each genre.

Plotting the action:

Plotting is important in storytelling: the plot is the arrangement of events that determines when and where characters face challenges and deal with conflicts; it includes the causes and effects of their actions, and how the story is resolved at the end. Within this design, we create suspense to grip the reader's attention.

Because real life is full of challenges and dilemmas, and our options for dealing with them are frequently constrained by other people's choices, there is hardly a nonfiction topic that does not involve conflict somewhere. And although we do not command a free hand to decide exactly what takes place when and to whom – as we would in fiction – two storytelling techniques enable us to create suspense and tension with factual material: 'foreshadowing', and 'controlled revelation'.

With 'foreshadowing', we drop hints of future events or implications before they happen, so that readers suspect things are not what they seem, or that the outcome is doubtful: they read on to find out. It can be done very simply: 'They decided not to lug the heavy radio equipment into the boat for such a short trip. That was their first mistake.' The subsequent account of the journey would build up to the point where readers become increasingly and worryingly aware of the need for the radio that the crew didn't bring. This method should be used sparingly – if hints are made about too many events, the technique loses impact and becomes predictable and tedious.

Another way to employ foreshadowing is to introduce characters briefly into the action before they play a significant role in the account, so that the reader is not confused by their sudden appearance, and you don't have to slow down the story to explain who they are; unless, of course, the suddenness of their appearance is a critical element of the narrative.

The second method – 'controlled revelation' – reveals the facts of an event a bit at a time, rather than all at once. The intervening text might be flashbacks or flash forwards, or descriptions surrounding the event.

For example, we might know that someone is dead, but not understand why. The reasons could be revealed gradually, building up through an entire chapter if this person was an important figure in the book. For this to work well, readers need to know in advance that the reasons are significant, and to engage sufficiently with the 'character' that they want to know the outcome.

Another approach is to introduce a problem or an uncertainty – e.g. about the arrival of something or someone essential, or doubts in reaching your destination, or recovery from an illness – but not to resolve readers' concern too soon. Let the reader fret over the situation for a while, building up tension. If solving the issue takes a long time, you will need to include occasional reminders of the problem and what is at stake. As with all these devices, be sparing in their use – subtlety has the greatest and longest impact.

A fictional story traces an arc: from the situation at the beginning, through the 'come and go' of the action, to the ending – the resolution. The end doesn't always tie up all the loose threads, or leave us with certainty, but it has to feel satisfying to readers: they are glad they kept reading.

In a well-written nonfiction book, part of the satisfaction is the quality of information it contains, and because real life is messy and continuous, tidy endings are not expected. But a narrative style can still create a satisfactory resolution in some form that gives meaning to the whole text. Depending on the genre, this might involve reflecting on the theme; considering how things might have been different; relating the content to other subjects or areas; updating to the present, or looking to the future.

Writing people and places as characters:

The presence of people in a book increases readers' interest and encourages them to engage with what they read. Every nonfiction book can include a human dimension: a text book on astrophysics could give brief sketches of scientists in that field and anecdotes about their squabbles. Even in academic writing, there is a move away from a strictly formal didactic approach to a more widely accessible narrative style.

Places, too, exhibit 'character' that inspire associations for readers; a strong sense of place can anchor a 'story' and fire readers' imagination. We make both people and places vivid and memorable in nonfiction by viewing them as 'characters' and using the techniques of creative writing. This doesn't mean we have no feelings for the people we write about, some of whom might have led tragic lives; instead, it helps us to portray people in ways that enable readers to better understand them and their situations.

Emotional involvement comes from stimulating readers' senses, and we can evoke them all – sight, sound, smell, touch and taste – in our depictions of places and people.

To help readers 'see' people more clearly, describe not only their actions, but their appearance; their clothes and how they are worn; objects they handle and keep around them; habitual gestures and other body language, and the way they walk. This is easier if you have your own observations or memories of people, but even for histories of an earlier period, go through your material carefully: you may find a surprising number of clues to this sort of information once you start to look for it.

Take advantage of imagery – metaphors and similes – when describing places, but sparingly, don't overdo it. Make them original: 'golden sunsets' are a cliché. A metaphor should produce instant visual recognition; it should provide a flash of insight, not an obscure reference that requires decoding.

We can help others 'encounter' places by describing characteristics of great significance for local people's lives: threatening volcanoes; avalanches; rivers that alternately sustain and destroy livelihoods; the scorching effects of hot, dry desert winds.

Sounds are evocative and create atmosphere: the slap and pounding of dough in a bakery may be the only indication of life in the pre-dawn silence. The rattle of harness, scuttering of mice behind a wainscot, or the distant tone of a cow bell, all bring your readers into the scene. People's speech patterns, stutters and accents add to their characterisation. In my high school, if the headmaster clutched his gown in front of him and coughed loudly through his nose, we all fell silent, knowing he was about to speak. Stretch your imagination to 'hear' small details which bring your writing to life.

Remembered smells bring people to mind, as well as situations: a pipe-smoking writer I once knew, whose signature odour of Old Vienna lingered long after his departure; the suffocating brew of smells that surround the very ill; the sweet-sickly scent of a young baby. All environments, manmade or natural, hold associated smells if you learn to recognise them.

To find ways of incorporating the sense of touch in your writing, you need to lose your inhibitions and free your hands. Some people are natural 'touchers', handling food and fabrics when shopping, and even running a hand over the chair they are sitting on.

Touch can indicate a lot about our surroundings: stone feels warm in a sunny place, dank and cold in perpetual shadow. Think of the objects people hold – do the same and note the sensation. If you're writing about the past, go to a museum and touch whatever exhibits you are allowed to – aware of the importance of this sense to deeper understanding, museums increasingly mount displays that can be handled – feel what an old leather bottle felt like to the person quaffing ale (do you need one hand or both to lift it?), or the lumpy scratchiness of a horsehair mattress to someone sleeping. These are all details which stimulate a reader's sense of 'being there'.

Are there people in your account who walk barefoot – either through custom or poverty? Take off your shoes, let your feet feel what theirs feel and you will experience a different way of describing the environment. And when you meet someone, notice how their skin feels when you shake hands – it is part of 'knowing' that person.

Taste is an obvious sense to excite if you are writing about food and drink, and they already claim a rich vocabulary of their own, although you should create more original terms where possible. But the significance of taste is not limited to gastronomy. Some indigenous African farmers put soil on their tongues to test its fertility, and the first deluge of monsoon rains on parched earth leaves the acrid taste of wet ash in your mouth. Travel writers who employ all their senses in exploring their surroundings enable readers to feel as if they are there, sharing the experience. The same applies to writing history that draws the reader into 'living' in a certain period of time.

Even in science, our empathy with a chemist's emotional intensity, in that moment before knowing his experiment is a breakthrough or a failure, is enhanced if we feel his hand grasp the fragile glass phial.

The more specific we can be, the greater pull we exert on the reader's attention: not a trail of 'scent', but of Lily of the Valley, or Tabu, depending on the person concerned. Search your data for suitable details.

Selecting tenses:

There are three main choices: present, past and future.

Present tense –

'He lifts the bike onto its stand.'
Or, 'Lifting the bike onto its stand, he calls out to me,' if he does two actions simultaneously.
'I step into the pub for a quick pint and see customers standing three deep at the bar.'

Past Tense –

'I walked to the cafe to meet Greg as planned, but he was not there.'
In addition, there is the 'past perfect' tense (previously called 'pluperfect'), which allows us to differentiate between the past event we are describing, and something that happened before it by using 'had', which avoids confusion and gives precision when needed.
The above example could mean that Greg was there earlier, or that he has not arrived.
If I want you to know which, I can use 'had' to say what happened before: 'I walked to the cafe to meet Greg as planned, but he had left/had not yet arrived.'
Confusion arises if a simple past tense is used when the past perfect is required:
'He learned to swing a club with skill before challenging his boss on the golf-course.'
This reads as if he learned this instantly, like superman, before walking onto the course. Using 'had' avoids this ambiguity:
'He had learned to swing a club with skill before challenging his boss on the golf-course.'

Future tense –

The words will/shall are inserted before the verb, but they imply different meanings which may be significant depending on the context:

'I/we shall go to the dance on Friday.' ('I'm just letting you know').

But 'will' is more emphatic: 'I/we will go to the dance on Friday.' ('Whether you like it or not'). It implies intent and determination rather than simply information.

Spoken to a second and third person, 'you/they', this difference is reversed:

'You will hurt yourself if you play with that cable.' ('I'm just warning you').

'You shall hurt yourself if you play with that cable.' ('I'll turn the power on to ensure you do!'). It implies a command or a promise.

Or, 'They will do their washing on Monday.' (An expectation or probability).

'They shall do their washing on Monday.' (An instruction or command).

This difference is recognised more in England than in other English-speaking countries, where it is often ignored; many people use either word freely but 'shall' infrequently.

I explain it here because the difference may be significant in documentary research, and it is important in contracts when specifying duties and options.

If a contract says: 'The agent will advise the author of any changes' – it is optional; the agent may do so.

If it says: 'The agent shall advise the author of any changes' – it is a duty and there will be penalties if it is not carried out.

The same difference is implied in 'would/should' when giving advice or instructions which you might need to give in your book:

'You would back up your work when you finish.' (A probability).

'You should back up your work when you finish.' ('I strongly urge you to do so').

And the much stronger statement:

'You must back up your work when you finish.' (The price for not doing so is great).

Which tense to apply in your book? The choice is yours, but there are implications to consider. Writing in the present tense gives a sense of immediacy, of the reader being present to observe, and from that perspective it is useful when you want to share your experience as it happens. I write in the present tense in travelogues for this reason. But present tense is harder to write fluently than past tense, especially if maintaining it for a whole book.

The critical thing to remember is not to mix tenses within one sentence, or within the same paragraph, otherwise you may confuse yourself as well as the reader. Switching tenses too often soon produces reader fatigue.

Making sentences:

Vary the length of your sentences to provide interest. Reading your work aloud enables you to pick up any awkward phrases that make you pause or stumble, and to hear the flow and rhythm of your words.

A sentence should contain a subject (who/which is doing something), a verb (what is being done) and an object (who or what is on the receiving end). Phrases (clauses) can be added into a sentence to tell the reader more about the subject, verb or object, or about where the action is taking place.

'A woman ran into the hotel foyer, which was crowded with tourists, grabbed the nearest person and yelled at him to call the police.'

Or, you could increase the drama by using a clause to describe the woman and only an adjective for the foyer.

'A woman, wearing only a negligee, ran into the crowded hotel foyer, grabbed the nearest person and yelled at him to call the police.'

Using both clauses in this sentence would overload it: make your choice according to your priorities.

Of course, it would be even more thrilling to write: 'A naked woman ran into the crowded hotel foyer…' But you are writing nonfiction – you must stick to the facts.

It is all right to employ more than one clause in a sentence, but the more clauses you include, the easier it becomes to entangle yourself and the reader. Separate clauses with commas, but when giving a list of items with descriptions, use semi colons to show that they are parts of a list rather than ordinary clauses, for example:

'The science library was comprehensive, containing documents on all aspects of biology; early discoveries in physics; on-going research on evolution, and recent advances in chemistry.' Note that the last item is separated only by a comma and the conjunction 'and', signalling that the list is coming to an end. When you read aloud, the tone of your voice lowers slightly to the conclusion of a sentence (unless you are Australian). Punctuation not only clarifies meaning, it guides you to read and speak a text with appropriate pace and rhythm.

It is acceptable to use a fragment – a phrase without all three elements – as if it were a sentence in order to emphasise a point: 'She had told the boys not to play footie indoors because if they hit the picture window it might shatter. It did.'

But you should not do this too often or the technique loses impact and becomes boring.

Group your sentences into paragraphs, each of which should contain one main idea with any descriptions, qualification or explanations that are required to understand your meaning. Paragraphs vary in length depending on the complexity of the central idea, but if you are writing specifically for an ebook, keep them short – about 100 words – because a long paragraph split over several screens in a digital reading device becomes difficult to follow.

Good grammar habits:

Syntax and punctuation are covered in greater depth in the chapter on editing, where you need it most, but some grammar tips are given here to help you develop good writing habits from the start.

Grammar is an interesting word. According to the Oxford English Dictionary, its origin goes back hundreds of years to the medieval French word for 'learning' – 'gramaire'. As magic and alchemy were important branches of knowledge, the word also meant 'incantation, spells and mumbo-jumbo'. This probably won't surprise you if you struggle with English grammar. But if we ignore the rules, we risk writing mumbo-jumbo ourselves and publishers are not impressed by that kind of originality. There is no magic to grammar – and not always logic – but if we follow correct practices, in time it becomes automatic.

Avoid wordiness – don't write more words than are necessary for clarity:

- The word 'of' is often a signal that we are doing this: 'The owner of the dog was walking beside the wall of my garden.' More concisely: 'The dog's owner walked beside my garden wall.'

- Parts of the verb 'to be' in conjunction with the 'ing' ending of a verb indicate a continuous action: 'I was sitting in the dentist's chair for two hours.' But this construction is frequently used unnecessarily: 'I am hoping it will end soon.' 'He will be wanting his dinner early.' Instead, write: 'I hope it will end soon.' 'He will want his dinner early.'

- Expressions common in conversation are not always correct in writing. For example, 'additional bonus' is tautology – it repeats itself. A bonus is already an addition. And in: 'definite decision', a decision is already definite. But note: 'irreversible decision' has a different meaning – more is at stake if a decision cannot be changed.

- 'At the end of the day' 'When all is said and done' 'When it comes down to it' 'Every once in a while' – are all empty meaningless verbiage. And if it is 'needless to say', don't say it.

Choose fresh, robust language – pay special attention to verbs and descriptions:

- Pick a strong verb instead of a weak verb plus an adverb. Instead of, 'She walked quickly along the corridor.' Write, 'She hurried along the corridor.' But stay realistic: only for an emergency would she have 'ran', 'dashed', or 'darted'.

- Choose vivid adjectives rather than insipid, overused ones, and shun 'really', 'very' and 'nice': 'He wore an elegant coat,' rather than, 'He wore a very nice coat.' 'We had a six-bedroom house,' is more descriptive than, 'We had a really big house.'

- Consult a thesaurus to increase your vocabulary, but make sure the meaning is appropriate: 'big' things may occasionally be 'immense' but few are 'colossal'. If in doubt, check the word in a dictionary.

- Avoid weak and woolly verbs like 'use', replace it with a more descriptive and explicit word whenever possible: 'I use (travel on/catch) the bus to go to work.' 'He used (employed/chose/applied) a different method of construction.' Or, change the sentence around to avoid it: 'She wrote her letter on airmail paper,' rather than, 'She used airmail paper for her letter.'

I suggest setting up a 'swear box' on your desk into which you pay a fine every time you write 'really', 'very' or 'nice': you might accumulate enough funds to help pay for editor's fees once the first draft is completed.

Keep it realistic – avoid exaggeration and physically impossible metaphors:

- Writing with vivid language means creating original images that make your subject come alive to readers, not writing 'purple prose'. Also called 'overwriting', purple prose uses descriptions and phrases that are over-elaborate, or exaggerated for the topic being discussed. For example: if a woman ladders her tights on her way to an interview, she is entitled to feel annoyed or even exasperated and we can sympathise with that. But 'her anger rose hot and bitter within her like a serpent ready to strike', seems excessive for a pair of tights.

- Keep your eyes in your head: a gaze or glance might wander or fall onto a plate, but it is extremely painful for eyes to do so. 'My eyes were glued to the road.' Ouch!

- Avoid obscure Latin words unless writing for obscure Latin scholars: 'sine qua non' simply means 'necessary'.

Other good habits:

- Try not to start every paragraph with 'there is/was/are', and think twice before writing 'it': this unspecified identity is ripe for ambiguity and confusion especially in longer sentences.

- Exclamation marks are strictly rationed: no more than one per 30,000 words. If you want to make an impact, shock or astonish us, do so with strong, vibrant sentences, not by inserting an exclamation mark to say: 'You're supposed to feel surprised by that.'

- Clichés require evasive action. They are usually the first expression we think of. If you recall a neat phrase you've heard before, it's probably a cliché: 'Over the top', 'A tall order', 'Off the radar', 'Something to die for' and 'Think outside the box'. Everyone understands them because they are catchy and popular. They are also as stale and tasteless as a piece of cheese that's been scudding around in the fridge for weeks. Don't feed it to your readers.

Quick tips for tricky bits:

- There/their/they're: 'there' is a place; 'their' indicates ownership; 'they're' is a contraction of 'they are' – the apostrophe here tells you the 'a' is missing.
  – 'They're waiting for their food, which I put over there.'

- Your/you're: 'your' indicates that something belongs to you – 'your style', 'your car'. 'You're' is a contraction of 'you are' describing you – 'You're late', 'You're an idiot'.

- Apostrophes also indicate possession: singly, a teacher's book is her property; in the plural, teachers' books are their property. But, when applying personal pronouns there is no apostrophe: it is yours, theirs, ours, his and hers, or mine.

- Its/it's: 'its' means belonging to it; 'it's' is a contraction of 'it is'.
  – 'When a tree sheds its leaves you know it's the beginning of winter.'

- Principal/principle: a principle is a fundamental law or moral attitude. A principal is the main or foremost of several items or people, like the boss. 'The college principal is my pal, but I condemn his infidelity on principle.'

- Stationary/stationery: think 'e for envelopes' and you'll remember that stationery is the one about papers and office supplies.

- Practice/practise: practise is a verb as in practising the violin, or practising medicine; practice is a noun, you can put 'the' or 'a' in front of it, the same as *ice*. 'It is a good practice to put ice in your drink to cool down after practising the salsa.'(Remember the 's').

- 'Awesome' means capable of inspiring awe and wonder; a 'fantastic' event is so extraordinary it could not happen in reality, and 'fabulous' is so incredible, it is the stuff of myths and fables. None of which is appropriate to describe the meal you ate last night or your new smartphone.

Before we leave the fantastic and fabulous, let's remind ourselves that we are writing nonfiction and it is worth thinking about the knotty problem of 'truth'.

In search of truth:

In his essay *The Prevention of Literature*, George Orwell wrote of *'the right to report contemporary events truthfully…'* – He was writing about literature in general as well as journalism, but it was 1946 and his main concern was loss of writers' freedom of speech under totalitarian states. We should be no less vigilant in democracies where spin-doctors massage the news and a small number of powerful monopolies control the media. But the other side of the right to tell the truth is the *duty* to do so.

Orwell's sentence continues: '...*or as truthfully as is consistent with the ignorance, bias and self-deception from which every observer necessarily suffers.*' Truth is not easily found. Irrefutable facts are few; everything beyond is someone's interpretation. About any one situation or event there are, quite legitimately, multiple 'truths' depending on whose perspective is expressed. History, in particular, has been prone to the bias of the victor and perpetuated through successive generations by text books following the same master narrative. Alternative histories of colonisation, for example, are only now emerging and receiving recognition.

Travel writers face the problem of their own cultural bias which screens both what they observe and how they interpret it. Writers of memoir and autobiography contend with the limitations of memory and the natural defences of self-deception; even writers of how-to and self-help books can tacitly not see potential weaknesses in their advice. Complete objectivity is not humanly possible.

Yet we seek in nonfiction to give a true account, not to make it up. That is its defining feature. To ignore that is to discredit not only the author, but the entire genre. So what can we do in our writing to be as honest as is humanly possible?

- Stay aware of our own particular potential for bias, and how our own values might influence our judgements in writing accounts of other cultures and times.

- Be meticulous in researching all sides of our topic, rather than finding only what we want to find. All good writing depends on selection – how much/how little to say – but selection is a judgement; if we claim to express principles of wider application, the criterion for selection should not be only the data that fits our cause.

- Enrich our writing by including other perspectives and other 'voices': acknowledging their truths while arguing for our own.

- Ensure we record accurately the information we glean from various sources, and take care to apply it without changing its original meaning.

- Make evidence-based facts more vivid by using story techniques like plotting, imagery and characterisation to tell *the* story, not build *a* story by manipulating dates and events, or leaving out inconvenient characters and facts. We can mislead and subvert truth by omitting something that is critical to the basic understanding of our subject.

- Do not fabricate. (Sadly, this is not 'needless to say': nonfiction writers are regularly exposed for inventing details, even people, in their articles and books. Succumbing to this temptation is usually a misguided attempt to strengthen their case, make their book more exciting or themselves appear more interesting).

All of this applies also to writing memoir and autobiography. But our inner truths are more difficult to access – we do so imperfectly – and they may cause anguish to the author and others involved. We should be as honest as we can in what we share, but we don't have to share everything. Deciding when the limit to disclosure has been reached is one of the most difficult facets of life-writing and why it is not reliable history, although reading memoirs can deepen our appreciation of other times and societies.

Up to now, I've discussed aspects of writing that apply to all nonfiction, but the next section contains further tips focused on specific genres. As before, in whatever genre you intend to write, I recommend you read the whole section: history is a form of travel through a different period; travel is a slice of your life. Describing a life requires a context in a past and a location – everything happens in place and time. Connectedness is the engine of creativity.

Writing tips for different genres:

Educational and text books:

I mention these first this time because the points of view, tenses and other parts of style that you choose, will depend on the age-range and learning level you are writing for, and especially on the requirements of any publisher or institution commissioning or using your work.

Within those constraints, it is possible to adapt many of the tips below to stimulate readers' imagination and to help them relate to your subject, whether it is geography, history, science or any other educational topic.

At the beginning of an illustrated history book written for young people, *Johannes Gutenberg and the Printing Press* (Twenty-First Century Books), Diana Childress begins by quoting a note written around 1385 by Geoffrey Chaucer in which he scolds his scribe, Adam, for making too many mistakes when copying his work: '*May the scalp under your long locks turn scurfy unless you faithfully write what I have composed.*'

From threatening dandruff and other frustrations of life before printing, the author moves swiftly on to describe Gutenberg's life and character – or what little is known of it – including human snippets such as a law suit brought against him by an upper class woman for breaking a promise to marry her daughter. Throughout the story of Gutenberg's invention and his first printing of the Bible, primary sources are quoted which give social and personal depth to historical facts. The book is part of an educational series, Pivotal Moments in History. The publishers, a division of Lerner Publishing Group, also produce geography books in a similar style.

Travelogues and guides:

Most travel guides are written in the present tense as impersonal statements of 'what is': 'The Wonky Towers Hotel offers cheap but tatty accommodation.' They might include past tense references from a first person point of view: 'I found the park became overcrowded during the evenings.' And future tense suggestions: 'If you walk beyond the ridge you will see splendid views.' However, a more formal guide would make a simple statement: 'The park becomes overcrowded in the evenings.' And, 'Beyond the ridge are splendid views.'

If you are writing for an existing series of guide books, or have been commissioned by a publisher to produce a guide, the style requirements will already be laid down and you should follow them. How far you can apply the following tips on writing travelogue depends on your brief and the purpose of the guide.

To write about your own travels from a third person point of view would be a strange choice, as it distances readers from your experience. But a 'third person' travelogue could be based on someone else's travels with the author as narrator, if the original traveller created sufficient information – journals, sketches, letters, and so on – for the author to reconstruct the journey, or to supplement it with contemporary material.

A first person account can be enhanced with others' observations quoted from conversations or interviews – perspectives given by a local guide, for example. Bear in mind your readers and your theme when deciding on point of view: why you are writing this and for whom. If your theme is broader than simply the journey or country itself – for example, following the boat passage of a group of asylum seekers – your own activities might be secondary to the refugees' stories, their conditions, and the background data and explanations.

Travel is generally written in the past tense. Present tense is difficult for inexperienced writers to sustain in a whole book, but that 'here and now' feeling that comes with using the present tense can be achieved in other ways. You could write in the past tense and include extracts from your journals or letters written in the present tense. Another possibility is to write some sections or chapters about particular events, in the present tense. By keeping these passages of present tense in discreet chunks, you avoid mixing tenses haphazardly in your main text.

The best travelogues are based on detailed journals, notes and recordings made at the time. Note as much as you can using all your senses, your feelings as well as actions and surroundings, especially things you know you will want to share later. Be sure to record days and dates, and the correct local spellings for names of people and places. For guidebooks, careful and detailed notes as well as local sources of information are a priority. Keep a list of local contact details so that you can double check or update facts later.

Quote dialogue to let us 'hear' the people you meet. Opportunities for humour in travel are numerous, but be sensitive to the danger of mocking others or being racist. The best laughs are usually against ourselves: the silly things we do and funny situations in which we entangle ourselves.

Make a locality's past more vivid by researching the people and stories that produced monuments, palaces, and other sites of interest that you visit, especially if they involve famous figures familiar to readers, such as Gaudi in Catalunya; Tamerlane in Central Asia; Pushkin in Moscow, and the Incas in Peru.

Include everyday small details characteristic of the area that can be compared to your own – forms of greeting for example. In Tibet, sticking out the tongue shows sincerity and goodwill because Tibetans believe that a black tongue conceals a treacherous heart. For the same reason, people in western societies shake hands with the right hand – traditionally the sword arm – so we cannot reach for our sword at the same time. But be alert for subtle differences between areas and sections of society.

Draw readers in to an appreciation of what is strange and different by linking it to something already within their experience. For example, mentioning familiar food and drinks can lead to how they are displayed in a local market; how they are eaten or cooked differently in their original settings, or how they are grown and harvested. The 'who, how, when, where and why' of a plate of sushi can open a window on social, geographical and historical features of a whole area.

Where appropriate, describe your own efforts at local activities. Perhaps you joined in a frog hunt, or tried weaving baskets; share actions and your feelings about them to enable readers to empathise with you.

Create metaphors and similes to help readers 'see' your descriptions, but make them original and not over-elaborate: they should project images that immediately mean something to a reader – preferably what you want them to mean.

Maintain the cultural flavour of your travelogue by using local names for objects (in italics) with the translation given afterwards, either in brackets or between em dashes like this: 'Crammed into a *tuktuk* – a three-wheeled motorised taxi – we could see little of the road ahead.'

Make sure each chapter is balanced between descriptions, actions, opinions and observations.

Readers need to know something about you and how you came to be in that location: it is part of your credibility and helps to reveal your own perspective on what you observe and describe. But it becomes tedious to read every detail of your planning and arrangements, unless these were fraught with special difficulties or are otherwise particularly significant. The same applies to the ending. We don't need to see you struggling through jet-lag on arrival and trundling your luggage home. Sometimes it's better to end a travelogue within your destination, perhaps with some insightful reflections.

In his classic travelogue, *From Heaven Lake*, Vikram Seth begins with an opening line that describes his immediate experience: '*The flies have entered the bus, and their buzzing adds to the overwhelming sense of heat.*' The rest of the long first paragraph describes, in the present tense, scenes the bus drives past in the town of Turfan where he begins his travels. In the last pages, while Seth sits in the plane bound for Delhi at the end of his expedition, he reflects briefly on his experience and, as an Indian, on the relationship between India and Tibet. After an amusing incident at customs, he ends his book with the sentence: '*I am home in half an hour.*' – A striking end to a land journey across China and Tibet that extended over two months.

In another classic, *The Old Patagonia Express*, the journey rather than the destination provided both theme and structure. Having finally arrived in Patagonia, Paul Theroux looks at the vast space around him and ends with two sentences: '*The nothingness itself, a beginning for some intrepid traveller, was an ending for me. I had arrived in Patagonia, and I laughed when I remembered I had come here from Boston, on the subway train that people took to work.*'

And in a more recent travelogue (2011), Jill Worrall, a New Zealand travel writer and tour leader, relates her experiences following ancient silk routes across Iran with an Iranian friend. *Two Wings of a Nightingale* (Exisle Publishing) is written from a 'first person' point of view, in the present tense, and is divided into twelve chapters, each focused on a different location, or section of the journey, describing their encounters with descriptive passages and dialogue.

The opening paragraph of the first chapter combines an ordinary activity familiar to us all, with an exceptional situation, suggesting a contradiction which attracts attention: '*We are pilgrims. We are pilgrims in the holiest city in Iran and we're trying to finish our saffron-flavoured ice creams quickly so that we can enter the shrine complex.*'

Histories:

People read history for two main reasons: to appreciate what life was like at a particular period – to experience 'being there' – and to understand where we are now, because history is not only about the past; it is the foundation of the present and always with us.

To achieve the first, we select elements of narrative style, of storytelling, to help readers identify with people, places and events of the past. To accomplish the second, we need elements of didactic style where the author is the narrator with the authority that comes from careful archival and documentary research. In historical writing, the author is not 'on-stage' in the same way that a travel writer is, and personal references – the use of 'I' – may be limited or absent altogether, but that does not mean the writing has to be dry and stilted.

Histories are usually written in the third person, recounting events that the author can 'observe' only through documentary evidence, but it is to some extent an omniscient view: the narrator can know everything within the limits of what has been recorded. Samuel Pepys wrote his thoughts as well as his sundry misdemeanours in his diary, so we can even reach inside his head. We cannot do the same for his wife Elizabeth: if she wrote a diary it has not been found.

However, there are ways we can achieve the closeness of a first person voice for parts of the text at least, if the right sort of material is available – finding the data is the key.

If you have access to correspondence and journals that relate to your theme, these could be quoted in the first person, letting readers hear their writers' voices, bringing them closer. Two-way correspondence has almost the quality of dialogue – but be careful that editing this does not change the content or sense of what was originally written.

It is rare for history writers to be able to draw upon interviews and actual dialogue for first person quotes, but if your topic is modern or local history, try to find people who lived through the episodes you are writing about, or perhaps had close relatives who did. Obtain first-hand information from them which can be written in the first person – so that they become additional storytellers.

Another possibility is for you to include sections in your book where you share with readers your site visits or museum research. Written in the first person voice, these passages would help readers to use all their senses in experiencing what you saw and felt inside an historic building, a ruin, or an archaeological dig, and what objects in a museum look, feel and smell like, and how they function – for example, if there is an ancient printing press that works, what does it sound like.

An original but more difficult approach to a tightly themed and focused history is to recount it in the 'first person' voice of someone who lived through that period, in which case, they would be the narrator. But it would have to be someone in a position to have personally seen a lot or who had access to factually correct information, and who left documents and diaries for the author to refer to as the source of information. Otherwise there would not be a lot of story to tell.

Many historical novelists employ this approach, but they are free to change dates and details, invent necessary additional characters or 'disappear' inconvenient ones which we are not. For a nonfiction book, this method has potential, but should be applied with care and a great deal of discipline.

The choice of 'character' as narrator is the critical challenge. In English history, for example, attempting an account of the Tudors from the point of view of one of Henry VIII's six wives has the limitation that, apart from the gossip of her ladies-in-waiting and letters from relatives, she would have little direct knowledge of events outside her bedchamber and the banqueting hall, and most of Henry's wives didn't last long in that position. Catherine of Aragon, his first, is the exception – she lasted twenty-four years as Henry's wife – and knew him intimately. She might have had sufficient access to affairs of state to tell a significant part of the Tudor tale – it depends what documentary evidence is available.

If information on a historical figure is mostly personal, it could only tell his or her story and might be better written as a biography than as a 'window' into the broader aspects of a period.

As one would expect, histories are generally written in the past tense, but a description of an author's site visit might create a sense of discovery for readers if written in the first person present tense. This is the stage to try out ideas for a page or two and see how it works. Much of the engagement in a history book is acquired through the author's deep immersion in the subject and the creative use of language to share that vision and enthusiasm.

Even within the strictures of accurate research, histories can be made more inspiring through storytelling: imagery for characterisation of people and place; plotting to create suspense, and resolution which conveys both meaning and a perspective on the past.

Judith Flanders could hardly choose a more sensational subject to write about than the Victorians' preoccupation with murder which she describes in *The Invention of Murder* (Harper Press). Her style includes all the narrative techniques we have looked at, applied to meticulously researched material. The text is accompanied by copious footnotes, end notes and bibliography, as she traces the projection of 'crime' into popular entertainment of the time, alongside the development of a police force and emergence of the detective novel. *The Invention of Murder* reads almost like a detective novel itself and opens with a gruesome quote and observations that encapsulate the entire enterprise:

'"Pleasant it is, no doubt, to drink tea with your sweetheart, but most disagreeable to find her bubbling in the tea-urn." So wrote Thomas de Quincey in 1826, and indeed, it is hard to argue with him. But even more pleasant, he thought, was to read about someone else's sweetheart bubbling in the tea urn, and that, too, is hard to argue with, for crime, especially murder, is very pleasant to think about in the abstract: it is like hearing blustery rain on the windowpane when sitting indoors.'

In *The History of Tibet*, Thomas Laird enlivened extensive historical data with interpretations from the most eminent spokesman for the country he could possibly have quoted – the Dalai Lama himself. And because Laird recorded all of his interviews with him, their dialogues thread through the book, making both the events and the character of the Dalai Lama vivid to readers

Memoir and autobiography:

Although an autobiography spans an entire life while a memoir represents a specific slice of that life, the same writing techniques apply to both.

You are the narrator writing from a first person point of view and, for the most part, in the past tense. But you can add variety by including reflections and updates in the present tense as separate paragraphs or sections; what you say will depend on the theme of your book but it will provide a thread of continuity running through the work.

Memoirs and autobiographies are not only about the author. Important elements of your story involve other people, their influence on you and your effects on them. Your feelings about them and your interpretations of their motives are a central part of the story, but remember, unless people express their thoughts directly, verbally or in writing, you cannot 'know' their motives. For this reason, and to draw the reader closer, include dialogue, quote letters, interviews, diaries (including your own) – anything that allows the reader to 'hear' what you heard. In the same way, give vivid descriptions of key people and their actions, good and bad, so that the reader, too, feels they know them and can empathise with your emotional response.

Early dialogue may have to be 'reconstructed', and memory plays tricks on us, but how you remember something is a valid part of who you are, the experience you are sharing and the effect it had on you. Where someone else, a sibling for example, remembers an incident differently, that is worth exploring because comparisons can deepen understanding of both the 'characters' and the experience.

One of the hardest parts of writing about our own lives is being as objective as possible. It is easy to romanticise or demonise the past. Include some snippets of research on social conditions of the time you are writing about to help yourself and your readers put situations into perspective. And describing your reactions to public events at the time, and how they affected you, gives a wider view of your life and provides common experiences to which others can relate.

Another way to broaden the appeal of a memoir is to consider the techniques of plotting described earlier. Creating suspense by the way you reveal events increases the tension in your story as it builds up to a climax. You can apply all aspects of narrative style, except pure invention, because it is a story you are telling – a true story. The resolution may leave some loose threads, as life invariably does, but explaining what you learned, or how you might have acted differently, can create a satisfying conclusion. It might also be an occasion for a brief updating epilogue.

As you write, keep in mind your purpose and readers – who you are talking to and why – because if you want it to be published, readers will expect to be stimulated and entertained as well as learn something of value. An entirely self-focused account becomes self-indulgent with little for others to identify with or learn from, and while it may be a valuable exercise for the author, it is better seen as therapy than a publishable book. However, this may be a stage you need to go through for your own sake before reviewing and rewriting from a broader perspective. The purpose – the choice – is yours.

Diana Athill wrote at least six memoirs – all written during her 80s – each with very different themes. Her latest memoir, *Somewhere Near the End* (published by Granta in 2009 when she was in her ninety-second year), has been the most successful. With a series of lively anecdotes, she describes what it is like to become old: the adaptations to physical limitations; activities relinquished (although she was still driving at the age of ninety-one); the smallness yet meaningfulness of each life and, inescapably, thoughts of what death might be like.

Despite its topic, it is an optimistic book. After a brief survey of various family deaths, she concludes: '*I have inherited a good chance of going fairly easily.*' In a society where old age is 'celebrated' and makes headlines only in its emulation of the young – 'Everest ascent by 85-year-old woman' – the appeal of this memoir seems to be the novelty of describing old age as it is experienced in reality by most people. In this respect, *Somewhere Near the End* seems well timed to fill a gap in the market.

An autobiography which vividly and accurately portrays the social and political history against which that life was lived, may still be popular years later as following generations seek their roots to understand the present and gain perspectives on the future. Es'kia Mphalele's second autobiography, *Afrika My Music*, originally published in 1985, is republished in South Africa in 2014 by Kwela Books, and catalogued as: '*Autobiography: Historical, Political and Military*' to reflect its broader relevance.

Biography:

A biography attempts the same depth and span of an autobiography, but from the distance of a third person point of view. Less data may be available, but where possible, quote first person accounts from letters, diaries and so on, both those written by the subject of the biography and by others who were involved in his or her life.

Most biographies are written in the past tense, but if the subject is living, or current results of their past actions are discussed, some sections would be in the present tense.

Social and political context is important, especially if the subject was a significant player; the selection and extent of social background depends on the life in question and the theme and focus of the biography – their career, the works they produced, or the impact they made in other fields. A skilled biographer blends tiny details of personal life into the broader picture of other contemporary lives and the spirit of the times. Peter Ackroyd defines this challenge in the introduction to his biography of Charles Dickens: '*To find in a day, a moment, a passing image or gesture, the very spring and source of his creativity; and to see in these details, too, the figure of the moving age.*'

Like memoir, a biography is a true personal story, but it is someone else's. And although narrative style increases the readability and enjoyment of a biography, objectivity and evidence-based data are the first priority. Inevitably, the author's judgements and interpretations are involved in its construction, but they are not the valid source of information they would be for autobiography and memoir. The author does not occupy a central role in a biography and elements of a more didactic style are appropriate. Reread the section on bias and truth before starting to write. Any personal or professional interest you have in the subject's life should be explained: colleague, relative, friend or foe.

Tap multiple sources wherever possible, especially for crucial parts of the 'story', remembering not to impute internal attitudes and motives to anyone. Biographers should examine their own motives, too, especially when deciding what to include or exclude. When intimate or sensitive information is available, consider whether its exposure is relevant and essential to the theme and purpose of the book, or merely titillates the reader or sensationalises the story. And bear in mind the earlier advice on libel.

Within these limitations, storytelling techniques, especially rich descriptions of people and places, will make your subject vivid and memorable. Scan your data carefully for expressions of emotion; childhood experiences, especially if they directly affect later life, and the subject's relationships with others. A deep and rounded account of a person's character, and influences that helped shape it, enables readers to relate to that person and gain greater emotional satisfaction, as well as insights into another life.

A common difficulty for biographers is access to primary data. Sometimes the information itself is limited, but the reasons for this may be turned to advantage. Little is known of Antoni Gaudi's personal life: there are few private letters; only brief notes in a diary maintained for a mere two months, and no confidences shared by this reclusive maestro obsessed with his work. The response of Gijs van Hensbergen in writing *Gaudi: a biography* (Perennial) was to accept that Gaudi lived through his architecture and that is where we can 'find' him. The author prepares us for this in the introduction: '*Gaudi's autobiography was written in stone; in broken tiles, tortoiseshell, twisted metal, stained glass and burnished gold; in cement and mortar.*'

The first comprehensive biography of Albert Einstein was published only in 2009, made possible by the release of Einstein's personal papers. In *Einstein: His Life and Universe* (Pocket Books), Walter Isaacson interweaves Einstein's chaotic domestic life, his freedom-loving nature, and a rebellious individuality, with the extraordinary energy of his creative genius. (Don't be misled by the name of the publisher: the book spans 700 pages).

Identifying how to make the best of available materials and staying informed about the release of documents are critical faculties for would-be biographers.

How-to, and self-help books:

Writers of how-to and self-help books share the aim of persuading a reader to take action resulting from the information and advice provided.

To achieve this, the author creates a close relationship with the reader, using a first person voice and addressing the reader as 'you' occasionally. Imagine your ideal readers sitting across the table from you and talk directly to them. Even a technical book that is more of a manual or handbook can be made more reader-friendly – and out-shine its competitors – by creating this relationship.

But practical instructions must be clear, concise, logical, and backed up with data that confirms their effectiveness. For these sections, the 'chattiness' of narrative style may give way to a more direct, authoritative teaching voice. Short paragraphs with bullet points achieve this transition well because the change of format alerts readers to note what follows. Think of it as clapping your hands to get everyone's attention. Subheadings such as 'Method', or 'Step 1', achieve the same result where appropriate.

Self-help books, particularly those in the mind-body-spirit category, share many of the characteristics of memoir; reading that section carefully may suggest ways of writing your own self-help title.

When sharing past experience, write in past tense; when giving instructions or advice, choose the present or future tense, but start a separate paragraph or section when switching tenses to avoid confusion.

If appropriate, increase the storytelling and vary the pace by including vignettes, anecdotes and case studies with fully-drawn characters and settings.

One of the most interesting cookery books I own (published over twenty years ago) is *Kaikai Aniani* (Robert Brown and Associates), a well-illustrated account of bush foods in Papua New Guinea. The author, R. J. May, details not only recipes, but where bush foods are grown; how to buy them in the markets; traditional and modern ways of preparing them, and a chart of their nutritional value. By way of entertainment, rather than practicality, one soup recipe – *Paua Sup* – begins: '*First catch your snake.*' So many once-exotic foods are now available in supermarkets worldwide, that anyone who has spent sufficient time in a region to appreciate its native cuisine might incorporate their travel experience in a cookbook of unique flavours we could all enjoy.

Timing – being attuned to people's current needs – is critical in choosing a successful approach to writing both self-help and how-to books. Amazon's number one best-selling cookbook (revised and republished in October 2013): *The New Artisan Bread in Five Minutes a Day: The Discovery That Revolutionizes Home Baking* promises to satisfy both the modern desire for crafted individuality in American eating, and the lack of time to achieve it.

Another timely publication, targeted at the popularity of both cookery books and thrift in New Zealand is Sophie Gray's *Feed the Family for $15 or Less* (Random House New Zealand). In addition to recipes, the book includes useful tips on shopping and menu planning that fit well with the theme, and are written with a touch of humour: '... *can be applied to any household budget, freeing up cash for other important things in life like debt reduction, education and handbags.*'

Getting Started:

The opening paragraph of your book can start anywhere, as long as it is intriguing, dramatic, unexpected or in some way compels the reader to keep reading. Think carefully about this launching point; even if the structure of the book is chronological, it needn't start at the beginning. Once your exciting event or startling disclosure hooks your reader, you can lead them back to the beginning in the next section.

But don't spend so much time agonising over this at the beginning that it inhibits you from starting: the ideal opening often comes to me after I've finished the first draft. If stumped, write 'Once upon a time' and proceed from there. Openings and endings receive more editing and revising than any other parts of a book. No one gets it absolutely right the first time and we will return to them in the chapter on editing.

Writing the first chapter can feel daunting. If you find yourself procrastinating unnecessarily, start somewhere else in the chapter outline. One of its benefits is to keep you on the right path wherever you happen to be.

Once you start, the mental stimulation of writing will spark ideas for other issues, or evidence that should be included somewhere in your book; don't be diverted by these, but don't lose them either: make a quick note on the timeline to follow up later.

Although we need to develop good writing habits as suggested earlier, these take time and a lot of writing before they become second nature. In the meantime, write freely while the sentences flow, without watching too critically over your shoulder; review and editing comes later – that is when the good habits are reinforced.

Try to establish a routine of writing every day, if only a single paragraph. You will soon find your rhythm. We all evolve our own rituals for switching to the 'write' frame of mind. I find that reading through what I wrote last time tunes me in to writing mode and helps me to pick up the scent of where I am in the text. It is much harder to start a writing session with a blank page in front of you.

What to do now:

→ Read aloud the 1,000-word article you wrote earlier and review it in the light of what you learned from this chapter. Make changes you think necessary, noting any bad habits you might already show, so you can look out for these in future editing. Save the article – it has more work to do.

→ With your chapter outline beside you, write two consecutive chapters of your book. They needn't be the first two in the outline, but they should be consecutive so that you try out writing the opening and closing paragraphs of both and the transition from one to the next. After writing, leave them alone for at least a week and work on other aspects of your book.

→ Read aloud and review the two chapters that have been 'resting'. Revise and check them for typos and errors, referring to advice in this chapter when necessary. (Main edits are carried out after the first complete draft of the manuscript and are described in Chapter 7).

→ Continue writing and reviewing two chapters at a time until your first draft is complete. Return here for advice, ideas and encouragement when you need it.

→   In between writing, continue with your research schedule and background reading.

→   And remember the mantra: save/print/back up after every writing session.

However committed we are to a project, we all become 'stuck' occasionally. The next brief chapter contains suggestions for what to do if you feel as if you are drying up or don't know what to write next.

And because the writing will continue for a considerable time, and we need to take breaks with other related activities to stay fresh, the next chapter also shows how to use time gaps in this extended writing period to begin establishing an online presence as an author: the status that will help you promote your book to agents, publishers and readers in the future. This is a gradual, long-term process, best started early with small steps.

6.

Maintain Momentum

Depending on how extensive your subject is and how much time you can devote to it, writing your book may take several months to a year or more, to complete. Suggestions in this chapter help you to maintain momentum and to profit from the intervening period by laying foundations for future promotion and marketing.

What to do if you feel stuck:

First, I want to dispel a favourite myth in writing circles: no such dramatic and life-threatening condition as 'writers' block' exists. Instead, tiredness, despondency and distractions can temporarily interfere with our inner desire to write.

Inspiration – creativity, the muse, whatever you choose to call it – does not arrive for our allotted writing session simply because we are sitting in front of a keyboard or a notebook: we must stimulate it. When your brain feels sluggish; you can't seem to find the words for what you want to say, or you feel as if your ideas are drying up, try the following:

- Write freely – don't inhibit your thoughts by trying to get every sentence perfect before you move on to the next. Remove the critic from your shoulder; reviewing and editing comes later.

- Read through previous writing – recapping on your last couple of pages jogs the memory to where you were last time the sentences flowed.

- Review some of your research material to re-immerse yourself in the subject and spark ideas.

- Start somewhere else in your chapter outline – read the outline and if any topic triggers thoughts and phrases, write about that. You can return to the previous chapter later.

- Write 200 words about any aspect of your topic to draw you back into 'talking' about it.

- Write 200 words about anything at all to tune in to writing mode. Just do it.

- Write in note form – if what you want to say is jumbled up in your mind and you are unable to order your thoughts or to form sentences, type them as rough notes to work on another day, or draw them as a mind-map with arrows to show how ideas relate to each other.

- List whatever distracts you at the moment. Place the list in a prominent place in another room or well away from your working space and return to your writing.

- Work on a less challenging task like listing the bibliography, constructing a glossary, tidying your filing system or browsing relevant web pages.

- Look at your photographs or illustrations for visual stimulation and write whatever thoughts they provoke.

- Read a novel or watch a video that is related to your subject but is informal and entertaining.

- Take a break – walk, exercise, increase your circulation and oxygen level.

- Stay cool – we are not machines. There is tomorrow.

Start building your author platform:

Establishing an 'author platform' involves taking steps to interact with people who share your interests, connecting with them and becoming known to future readers, contacts, collaborators and colleagues in your writing venture. Like all social processes, it requires the gradual development of understanding and mutual trust. And the practice is on-going: relationships are only as strong as their last reciprocation – they need to be maintained.

If you move to a new location, it takes time to meet people, join clubs and organisations, follow up contacts, participate in local events and find those who share your aims and passions: networks through which you give and receive encouragement, support and stimulation. Your new writing project offers similar possibilities: the library might know of a writers' or readers' club; you could offer to share your expertise by talking to a school, college or relevant interest group. But to become more widely known as an author, it is necessary to forge these links in the virtual world of the Internet, in addition to your physical environment.

It is hard to be visible in a world where thousands of new books are launched every week. Agents and publishers expect writers to create their own platforms; to build up, interaction by interaction, a 'stage' to stand on which raises their heads above the crowd to see and be seen, and to achieve this before their book is launched. Although your author platform is the foundation for future marketing and promotion (which I discuss in detail in chapter 9), the aims, procedures and time-scale are different, which is why you need to start now. Developing a following of interested people is a long-term endeavour: without this base, no one will be watching when your book is released.

In addition to joining in the community around you, learn to participate on websites, blogs, and social-media. This is where readers and professionals gather to share their views and exchange information, and where writers not only show their work, but learn more about their subjects, their readers and the publishing world generally. The Internet is a notorious thief of time: you need to establish a strategy and pace yourself.

My own strategy is to promote my website in conjunction with Twitter, rather than attempting to spread myself (and my time) over many different social media sites, and I recommend this as a good way to start, especially when you are in the middle of writing a book and pressed for time.

If you don't yet operate a website or a blog, setting one up can wait till nearer the completion of your manuscript, but engaging in social media should begin now, so that when you are ready to post news of your book on your own blog or on someone else's, you have followers to tell. No one knows you run a blog, however superb it may be, unless you employ a means of directing people towards it. The chances of anyone coming upon your site among the thousands of new ones launched daily, is extremely remote without social media promotion and an audience that is already listening.

I post articles regularly – usually weekly – on the blog page of my website and interact briefly, but daily, on Twitter. The community of writers, readers, journalists, agents and publishers on Twitter is huge and diverse. I consider it the best forum for writers to make contact with like-minded people; find relevant websites; interact with those who share an interest in their subject, and access resources.

For those who are new to Twitter, the following notes will enable you to make the most of the opportunities it offers. Over the last few years of Tweeting, I have learnt an enormous amount about a range of topics and found lots of inspiration by following links shared by others. I have also forged mutually productive contacts and created genuine friendships.

Making the most of Twitter:

Access www.twitter.com on your computer; click on 'About' right at the bottom of the screen, and in the second paragraph of the introductory page that comes up, click 'see it in action' to view a brief video of someone using Twitter. In less than two minutes he sees an interesting tweet; accesses the link; sends a short tweet of appreciation, and interacts with several people about his message.

Setting up your profile:

On the Twitter website above, click on 'sign up' and follow the detailed instructions.

Twitter users (variously called Tweeters, or Tweeps), are identified by a 'Twitter handle' – a name prefixed with @ which makes it a live link with access to their profile page and tweets. The purpose is to become known, so sign up with your own name. Don't be surprised if others among the millions of Tweeters share your name and have already bagged it – use dashes, numbers, abbreviations or initials to create a unique handle. You can add 'writer' or 'author' to your name if you wish, but a long name takes up space in a tweet: only 140 characters are available, and you need to leave room for others to respond to you.

If your blog or website is like your office – a professional place of work/entertainment to which you invite new contacts, colleagues, clients and friends – your 'Twitter Profile Page' is the brass plaque beside the office door; it shows who you are, what you stand for and what you are interested in, so choose your photograph and profile description with care. If you put almost nothing in your profile and remain an 'egg' (default image in the absence of a picture or avatar) people will think you are a spammer or a Bot and avoid you. Become familiar with the options and settings on your profile page – you can edit your profile at any time.

Finding people to 'follow':

Until you follow a few score people you will appreciate little of how Twitter works because you will see too few tweets. There are many ways of finding suitable people whose tweets you'd want to read:

- Twitter suggests people to follow on your Profile Page but check them out first (see 'Checking' below).

- Insert 'hashtag + topic' (e.g. #history #travel #memoir) in the search window to see who is tweeting on that topic; click on their Twitter handles and see who they are and the sort of tweets they send.

- Click Twitter's 'Who to follow' buttons and check out any that look suitable.

- Go to an interesting Tweep's Profile Page and click on 'following' in their profile to see who they are following, and pick some of those.

- Check out people that follow you and decide whether to follow back (avoid spammers offering 'get hundreds of new followers').

- Tweeps with roughly even numbers of 'followers' and 'following' are more likely to follow you back, but there are people whose tweets you might like to keep up with, even though they are unlikely to follow you in return.

Checking potential followers:

Click on @handles, and click again to get their full profile and timeline. Scroll through to see what they tweet (if it's all self-promotion, swearing, racism or just silly, I don't follow). Click on their website (if they have one) and see if it interests you.

If you regret following someone, no problem, you can 'unfollow' at a click.

Seeing tweets you want to read:

The more people you follow, the greater number of tweets stream down your timeline and it is easy to miss ones you particularly want to see, especially if they are in a different time zone to you. You can pick up these tweets by creating a 'List' – click the little 'cog-wheel' on the header of your Profile Page and follow the menu for 'lists'. Then go to the Profile Page of a Tweep you want on your list, click on the 'head silhouette' and select 'add to list'. All their tweets will appear in your list whenever you choose to look at it, without having to spend too long watching the main stream. You can list a Tweeter without actually following them, and construct as many lists as you wish.

Another time-management technique is to use the 'Favourite' button underneath a tweet. If you see a tweet you want to check later, a link you'd like to read another time, or a Tweep you want to keep note of, click on 'Favourite' and it will be saved in the 'Favourites' heading on the left panel of your Profile Page for as long as you wish. To delete it, click 'Favourite' again and it will disappear.

What to Tweet:

Take your time. Observe others for a few sessions and find your bearings. Until you tweet, no one knows you are there, watching and listening like a ghost at a cocktail party.

- You don't have to tweet every day or make profound, earth-shattering statements in every tweet – you only have 140 characters anyway, you can practise concise writing. Share snippets of information about your subject (but be careful not to tweet your book), and comment on interesting posts.

- Aim to balance giving helpful content and supporting others, with your own promotion e.g. tweeting links to your blog posts.

- A general rule of thumb is to work in thirds – a third of your tweets re-tweeting or passing on useful links or information, including links to your own blog; a third on comments/observations about your life, work, environment, or inspiring quotes that may be of general interest, and a third responding directly to other Tweeps (i.e. using their @handle) in brief chats, congratulation, encouragement; remember, you are 'talking' to real people with feelings and opinions.

- Re-tweeting (RT) another's message is helpful to them. But make sure you understand what you are passing on, and always check a link before re-tweeting it, to make sure it works and contains information you would want your followers to read.

- You can RT by clicking the 'retweet' button beneath the tweet, or be more interactive: click 'reply', copy and paste the original message and add a few words of your own followed by 'RT' in front of the sender's handle. This is more likely to generate responses and potentially interesting 'conversations'.

- When writing your own tweets, don't take up all 140 characters. Leave at least 30, so that others can add their own comment when they RT – e.g. 'Brilliant!'

- If you change anything in a message you want to re-tweet – to make space for a comment for example – it is courteous to add MT instead of RT to indicate you modified the original.

- If people RT your messages, respond and thank them.

- And remember to check your 'Connections/Interactions' stream regularly to reply to those sending you @ messages or re-tweeting you.

Hash tags (#):

- #FF or #ff stands for 'FollowFriday', and precedes the @handle of Tweeps you want to recommend your followers to follow. Tweeps use it loosely as a 'Happy Friday' greeting, and long lists of automatically generated names are meaningless, but applied with discernment it can forge relationships and networks. Done properly it is time-consuming and I don't do it very often – but it's a good way to thank regular re-tweeters and particularly helpful Tweeps.

- #WW stands for 'Writers Wednesday' to greet and acknowledge other writers. I don't have time for this, but always thank those who acknowledge me.

- Twitter gathers hash-tagged tweets and displays them in an additional separate stream. If you enter hashtag + topic in the 'search' window of your Profile Page, you see a list of recent tweets and people related to that topic, e.g. #writing #food #health. These are useful to attach to a tweet for which you want extra attention, because it will be seen by others who do not (yet) follow you, e.g. when promoting blog posts on my trip to Porto, I added #travel #Portugal

- Use hash-tags sparingly because they are 'live' in the message and come out paler, making it hard to differentiate from a web link: too many make the tweet hard to read.

Security:

Just as you would lock your car, not leave your purse on the shopping trolley while browsing in the supermarket, or accept sweets from strangers:-

- Create a strong password – at least 6 characters in a mix of upper and lower case and numbers – and change it from time to time.

- Always log-out before turning off (from the dropdown menu of that little 'cog-wheel'), so your portal into Twitter is not accessible to anyone else.

- Be wary of links tweeted directly (@) to you by non-followers, especially if they are not following anyone and/or display no profile. These links are usually viruses, spam or otherwise objectionable and you can block the senders or report them for spam. It doesn't happen often, but they tend to target new users.

- Block tweeters you don't want following you by clicking on the silhouetted 'head' of their profile page and using the dropdown menu – from here you can block or report 'bad guys' for spam, or enter the 'good guys' into your lists.

- Anyone you are following can send you a Direct Message (DM) which is 'private' (but never assume anything over the ether is truly private). This is useful for networking with Tweeps you have come to know and trust, or to exchange email addresses for further discussion. But sometimes new followers send automated promotional links via DM. I ignore or delete such unsolicited DMs.

- If you get a DM – even from a known and friendly Tweep – with a link and message like 'they're saying bad things about you here' or, 'you won something', or, a new one, 'terror attack in [US city of your choice] 4,000 killed' do not open the link, delete the message. These are viruses sent by someone who has hacked a Twitter account and sent this message to all its followers. Unfollow the Tweep and tell them their account is hacked. It doesn't happen often, but they tend to target new inexperienced Tweeps. If your account gets hacked, change your password. If you follow proper security it shouldn't happen to you.

- Some people never check their DMs, so if you need to send one, it is advisable to tweet the recipient that you are doing so.

These are a few suggestions to help you start. You will learn more by using Twitter and discovering what the different 'buttons' and short-cuts offer, along with a range of programmes and Apps that can help you manage your Twitter account. Read the small print and exercise the same caution in registering for these as you would for any other unfamiliar website.

Creating an author platform is not something you can do alone: it is essentially a collaborative enterprise. We earn the attention and loyalty of others because we are sincere in returning them. Through social media you can promote your book in moderation and in subtle ways, but Twitter is not a sales counter. If you accumulate 1,000 followers, perhaps 30% of them see your tweets regularly (especially if they put you on a list); it is not possible to interact even occasionally with more than 20% of those (unless you spend all day tweeting), and of those 60 people, perhaps 10% will buy your book at some point in the future and perhaps recommend it to their friends.

Treat social media as a tool, alongside others, for the long-term development and maintenance of your reputation as a writer and a person. The response we gain from others is directly related to the quality of what we give.

What to do now:

→ Print out the page on what to do when you get stuck and put it somewhere where you see it from your desk: it is when we are stuck that we forget such tips.

→ Look around your community for opportunities to take part in groups or events related to your subject and/or your writing.

→ Identify useful websites, blogs and online writing forums, either to participate or to refer to as sources of information and encouragement.

→ Open a Twitter account and take your time learning how to gain the most from developing a social media presence.

→ Keep writing.

→ Read the Social Media section of Chapter 9 for guidance if you decide to set up a website or blog now rather than later.

7.

Edit Your Draft

E diting is less about picking up mistakes and more about developing your manuscript to its full potential. It is simply the next step in the process of writing. All writers, however experienced or however many books they have had published, need editorial feedback on their writing because, although we revise, we are too close to assess our own work. We need the eyes of an experienced reader of the genre to make sure we have actually written what we think we have written. Saying what we mean is not as easy as it might seem.

Agents, and publisher's commissioning editors, will consider the overall idea and theme of your manuscript to appraise whether, for them, it is marketable. If they think it is, their own copy editors will examine the text and suggest further changes and corrections. These will be based not only on the manuscript's quality, but also on the house style of the publisher and the requirements of the market to which they aim their books.

But they won't waste time on a first draft: unless you have carried out your own revisions and followed that up with external editing, your manuscript will not get as far as an agent's or publisher's desk.

Carrying out your own review and revisions –

Writing and revising involve separate mind-sets; treat them as two different parts of the project. When your first draft is complete, put the manuscript away for at least a couple of weeks, so that you read it with a fresh perspective. I find it easier to edit from a hard copy, and to move away from my writing desk to a different location.

Rather than try to look out for everything at once – and miss problems – I review systematically in two stages, assessing different aspects in each. Revising is as important as writing and deserves time and thoroughness.

Revising for structure:

Stage one of revision focuses on structure, flow and development of ideas –

This one is the most critical review because no amount of later polishing will correct a structural weakness. It's not the repainting of the Forth Bridge that holds it together, but the design of its struts and arches. At this point, the effort put into your chapter outline brings its rewards: if you followed a carefully laid plan, returning to adjust the route where necessary, fewer revisions will be required.

Read straight through your manuscript and mark up any places that lack any of the following:

• Within each chapter, an enticing opening that leads straight into the main issues; followed by a build up of those ideas or actions to a concluding paragraph compelling the reader to continue.

• Transitions effortlessly carrying the reader from one chapter to the next. While chapter openings and endings need significance or drama, they also link chapters so that the reader is saved from "Where am I?" or "How did I get here?" confusion. If you included flashbacks, or started later in the story to work back to the beginning, check these are woven into the text and the chronological span of your narrative is clear.

• Logical sequences and development of ideas within paragraphs. In general, each paragraph should focus on one main idea, which evolves by plausible steps to its climax in the last sentence. To test this, try summing up the central point of your paragraph in half a dozen words. If you can't, consider splitting it into two.

• Smooth flow of ideas that lead through one paragraph to the next. Paragraphs vary in length to the rhythm of what you are saying – explanation or emphasis – and such variety avoids reader fatigue, but, like chapters, they need transitions. If you can't find a way to create a fluent transit between two paragraphs, one of them should probably be moved somewhere else, or is unnecessary.

- A feeling that the account is complete and balanced: neither too little, nor too much of any facet, and nothing significant left out. We are all tempted to give our favourite topics more space than is warranted in the overall scheme. Refer to your outline to keep a sense of proportion and be prepared to cut (rework the material later for articles or blog posts).

- Statements and claims are correct and make sense – is there enough supporting data, or are there unjustified assumptions? Does anything need re-checking? And look for bias: places that leave out evidence, or other points of view that are critical to a full understanding of your subject. Consider whether large chunks of data, or extensive supporting material, might be better in an appendix.

- Content that explores the theme. If material has nothing to do with your theme, or does not feed into the arc of your narrative, it should not be there, however entertaining or pleasing it may seem.

- A satisfying conclusion that reflects your stated intentions at the outset. Potential endings are as diverse as the topics we write about, but readers should be left feeling they learned something of value from your book and that the time spent in reading it was worthwhile.

Once you have revised the entire manuscript for structure and content, you appreciate the arc of the enterprise, drawing out its theme and ideas from the beginning and building them up to the end. This is the time to rewrite the opening paragraphs of your first chapter – the hook that catches the reader's attention. But the hook must not dangle in isolation: the bait comes from some vital part of your story and is attached to the line that reels readers in to the rest of your narrative.

Examples of opening paragraphs:

I quoted a few openings in the section on writing for different genres, but here are others. You can add to them with your own reading to help you decide what kind of opening would best draw readers into your subject.

'*Being a peasant during the Middle Ages must qualify as one of the worst jobs in history – but then we're only guessing because the peasants didn't leave much record of their lives. Except once, in the summer of 1381, when they left an indelible mark on the history of England.*' The reader's interest is roused as to what this indelible mark was, and the next paragraph begins a lively description of the 'peasants' revolt'. (*Medieval Lives*).

'*Antoni Gaudi Cornet was born as he died, untidily – the subject of controversy.*' The use of 'untidily' is unusual in references to birth and death – the reader's curiosity is piqued and further drawn with a promise of controversy. After this extremely brief opening, Gaudi's 'untidy' birth takes up the second paragraph. (*Gaudi: A Biography*).

'*On the evening of 16 September 1849, Edgar Allan Poe stopped in the office of a physician in Richmond, Virginia – John Carter – and obtained a palliative for the fever that had beset him. Then he went across the road and had supper in a local inn. He took with him, by mistake, Dr Carter's malacca sword cane.*' The events here are told like a storyteller; we know a tale will unfold, and the possible role of the Malacca cane – such an odd detail – makes us want to read the rest of the story. We are not disappointed: the rest of the chapter continues with Poe's fateful and mysterious last journey. (*Poe: A Life Cut Short*).

'*In Alice Springs – a grid of scorching streets where men in long white socks were forever getting in and out of Land Cruisers – I met a Russian who was mapping the sacred sites of the Aboriginals.*' The amusement of this description is matched with the surprise of a Russian in that context and encourages readers to find out more. The remainder of the chapter introduces this most unlikely of guides who accompanies Bruce Chatwin on his Australian travels. (*The Songlines*).

'*Everything has been globalized except our consent. Democracy alone has been confined to the nation state. It stands at the national border, suitcase in hand, without a passport.*' The provocative first line, and the vivid metaphor of entrapped democracy, starkly outline George Monbiot's theme: because of the uneven distribution of global power wielded by a few, a small number of men, in effect, control our lives. (*The Age of Consent*).

Both theme and title of Mamphela Ramphele's recent book, *Conversations with My Sons and Daughters,* are drawn together factually and symbolically in her opening paragraph that begins with part of a conversation spoken by a young man – quoting a traditional phrase still relevant – and encompasses the message of her book in a nutshell:

'Mabu a u tswitswe! *These words haunted me for a good week or so. They were uttered early in 2011 by a young professional man with a pensive look on his face.[…]This Sepedi idiom – which literally means 'the soil has been stolen' – is used as a call to action to defend the land following the assassination of a king by a conquering power.'*

The sons and daughters are figurative – referring to the youth of South Africa – whom Ramphele addresses as an elder talking across the generations, issuing a rallying cry to regain the dreams of a post-apartheid South Africa which are slipping away through the political, economic and social ills of the present.

In the following opening paragraph to a self-help book, author Amanda Stuart intrigues us with a brief description of real people showing signs of emotion to which we can all relate, and she adds her own feelings.

'*They start arriving, looking apprehensive, edgy, smiling at one another weakly. It is obvious some have slept badly and look fragile. I feel pleased to see them, proud of them for taking a risk with no idea of what the weekend holds in store, knowing only that they are here because they want to make a difference to how they feel about their lives. They want to bring about change.'*

References to risks and personal change lead directly into the theme of her book: the long-term effects of childhood trauma and the benefits of counselling. Considering the sensitive nature of personal case studies contained in the account, a more dramatic or sensational opening would have been inappropriate. (*The Longest Journey*).

Revising for language and clarity:

Stage two of revision looks at language for clarity and rhythm –

Both are related to grammar and sentence construction, so rereading those sections in Chapter 5 will tune you into the right thinking mode.

To sustain your momentum through this slow task, approach one section or chapter at a time, with breaks in between.

Remind yourself of your statement of purpose, readers and theme, and read the manuscript aloud this time as you bear in mind the following questions, marking up passages that spark any doubt in your mind:

- Is the language – words, images and complexity of sentences – appropriate for your readers? Plain words and simple syntax produce clarity, intensified with original imagery and active verbs. Avoid repetition of words by selecting the one that bears your exact meaning in each case. Scrutinise adverbs and adjectives and replace them with stronger verbs wherever possible.

- Is the writing concise? Look out for wordy or unnecessary phrases. Verbal clutter is tedious to read and hides the important points. Delete not only the common culprits but also superfluous words – check afterwards the meaning is still clear. For example, the word 'that' can often be cut but is sometimes essential to avoid ambiguity, especially before or after a verb.

- Does it read fluidly? Note places where you stumble or hesitate. If a long, unusual or difficult-to-pronounce word makes you pause, replace it with another that flows easily off the tongue.

- Are there too many clauses? This can leave a reader struggling in a swamp of words, especially if verb and subject become widely separated. Longer sentences are more suitable for a slower pace, shorter ones when you want to gain momentum – for example, towards a climax in the narrative.

- Are clauses ineffectually tacked on to the end of sentences? Look out for clauses that have moved so far away from the core point of a sentence that they should be split into a new sentence, or be separated by a semi-colon. Sometimes a punch-line packs more

115

impact as a separate short sentence than as the last clause in a long one. (See further notes on clauses below).

• Are tenses, points of view and narrator's voice consistent within each section or chapter?

• Do any passages feel over-written: appear too elaborate or exaggerated for what is being described? If so, simplify with more appropriate images. Fuller descriptive prose is best placed where the pace is intended to slow, allowing readers briefly to rest and reflect. But trim it back wherever your narrative gains pace to build up to a crucial point in your argument.

Further notes on clauses and punctuation:

Clauses, like small puppies romping in a room, can trip us up unexpectedly. And like pups, they come with two distinct characters: dependent and independent.

A clause contains a single, complete idea. It is 'independent' if it can stand alone, i.e. it could also be a sentence. For example, 'I wrote my first chapter and filled eight pages,' consists of two clauses joined by 'and'. The first clause could stand alone as a short sentence. The second clause also contains a single idea but does not make sense on its own. It is 'dependent' on the first clause to tell us who the subject is and what the action is about.

I could add another dependent clause using the conjunction 'with': 'I wrote my first chapter and filled eight pages with surprising ease.' Or the independent clause could be separated with a comma instead of the 'and': 'I wrote my first chapter, filling eight pages with surprising ease.'

Clearly, two dependent clauses cannot make a sentence, but two independent clauses can.

Both 'writing a book is a long journey' and 'we need a guide' are independent clauses that could each make a short sentence. As the two ideas are closely related, they could also be combined into one sentence, but because they are independent, we need something stronger than a comma to hold then together. Using a comma to separate two independent clauses or to add one on the end of a sentence is called a 'comma splice' – like a join made with sticky tape, it doesn't provide a strong enough structure for the sentence.

Instead, we usually join them with a semicolon: 'Writing a book is a long journey; we need a guide.' Or with a dash to indicate a thought that follows on from the previous one: 'Writing a book is a long journey – we need a guide.' And because the second clause in this example expands the first statement, I could give it more impact by using a colon: 'Writing a book is a long journey: we need a guide.'

There are probably ten ways of constructing a sentence around any given idea, each arrangement of words and phrases providing subtle changes in meaning, emphasis, impact and rhythm. These different ways to punctuate and link clauses allow us to add variety, which is fortunate because the too-frequent repetition of semicolons, dashes and conjunctions becomes tedious to read. Remember, the two main purposes of punctuation are to achieve clear meaning and fluid reading.

For the same reasons, we vary the length of sentences from one independent clause (to emphasise a point), to several clauses (to enlarge ideas or descriptions). A whole paragraph of one-clause sentences lurches like a car driven by a learner driver stepping on the brakes too often.

With practise, we learn to drive smoothly through complex sentences, decelerating (adding commas) between clauses, and knowing when to touch the brakes lightly (with a semi-colon, colon or dash) or to brake firmly at a full stop. The pauses and stops are part of the rhythm of our writing style, but above all, they enable readers to grasp the full meaning of what we write. When we speed on through long sentences, adding clause after clause with only commas to separate them, we move too far away from the core meaning of the sentence, and readers are rushed past ideas without fully appreciating them.

One further important aspect of dependent clauses is that they can disrupt the meaning of a sentence, according to where they are placed. Remember that a dependent clause 'depends' for some critical component – the verb, subject or object – on the main or independent clause. A poorly positioned dependent clause can attach a description or action to an inappropriate object or subject, making nonsense of the sentence. For example, 'After waiting several months, Sonya finally received her manuscript from the editor with torn edges and stains.'

No doubt editing can cause physical stress, but it is the manuscript that was torn and stained, not the editor. There are several possible ways to fix this problem, but as Sonya was likely to feel indignant about this outcome, I would add emphasis by using a semicolon or a full stop: 'After waiting several months, Sonya finally received her manuscript from the editor. The document was torn and stained.'

Many people experience difficulty with grammar and syntax. If you are one of them, I recommend you select a basic grammar from your local store. A good bookshop will stock several, so before you buy, examine the book to make sure that the explanations and layout are easy for you to follow.

After editing, you can give a final polish to your manuscript by searching for words that you depend on too often, or for common problem words like 'it' that may create ambiguity. Select the 'Find' function from the tool bar and enter, for example, the word 'use'. By successively clicking 'Find Next' you will see every instance where you wrote 'use': consider each one and decide whether it is the most explicit and descriptive verb available in each context. Repeat the task with 'it' and check that the meaning is clear and unambiguous in each case. Try the method with others of your 'favourite' words – it is a disturbingly revealing exercise.

Other tasks to work on during breaks in revision:

Maintain momentum during breaks between revision sessions, or when your manuscript is 'resting', by tackling other tasks that can be achieved incrementally and provide you with a change of pace. Another reason for working on them at this stage is that you now see the whole narrative in perspective, enabling you to make better decisions.

Chapter headings:

Having reviewed your structure, this is also a good time to revise your chapter headings to make them inviting and informative.

Introduction:

Write the first draft of your book's introduction; it is likely to be redrafted several times between now and publication, but you will have formed a foundation for further work.

The introduction might contain guidance on how to use the book; reasons why you wrote it; comments about the subject in general, or a brief outline of what to expect. However, it should not include any background or explanation that ought to be somewhere within the body of the work. Some readers pay scant attention to introductions.

Consider whether or not you should include a prologue and/or an epilogue (these were discussed in the section on Creating Your Chapter Outline). If one or other is essential, write it now.

Illustrations and photographs:

Source and select the illustrations, photographs or other art work you wish to include. Ensure the captions for each are accurate. Double check spellings, dates, names and sources, but it is inadvisable to quote captions in the text at this stage: only when preparing for publication will you know how much art work will be included and where it will be located in the book. Printing images is expensive, so you will have to prioritise your choices, and tables do not convert well for many digital formats – you might have to find other ways of showing that information.

Appendices:

Assess whether appendices would be helpful to readers: historical timelines, maps, glossary of terms, case studies, interview transcripts, or other original data, for example, and if so, begin working on them. Continue compiling a bibliography or suggestions for further reading.

Proofreading:

After your own revisions are completed and before sending the work for external feedback and editing, you should proofread the manuscript to pick up any typos, spelling or punctuation errors and formatting misalignments. This is a painstaking task because, when we read, the brain automatically 'corrects' errors, showing us what we expect to see. The difficulty is compounded with our own writing because we already know what is supposed to be there, (for this reason, the final proofreading before publication should be carried out by a professional proof-reader).

If you are a sub-vocal reader – you 'pronounce' words in your mind when your read – you will find errors more easily; habitual speed-readers have to adopt a close-reading style. To avoid skimming down the page and overlooking mistakes, lay a ruler under each line and examine individual words. Look out for the following common typos and transpositions: their/there/they're; where/were/; than/that; the/a; he/the; at/an; too/to/two; loose/lose; is/are; then/than; hte/the.

Making changes during revision often leaves a trail of small errors: single versus plural; misplaced apostrophes; verbs and nouns in different tenses; joining words – and, but, which, although – inadvertently left behind when re-styling a sentence. Always check the text after any editing.

Where more than one spelling is possible – such as learnt/learned, Jane/Jayne – check that the same spelling is used consistently throughout. The same applies to units of measurement: miles or kilometres, metres or feet, pounds or kilos. If quoting both miles and kilometres with one in brackets, for example, make sure the same one is always bracketed. For historical dates, whether using BC/AC or BCE/CE do so consistently through the text.

Be extra careful around figures – check the number of zeros and whether decimal points are in the right places – and with the spelling of foreign words (which should be in italics unless in common usage in English such as 'cliché', for example).

And remember: spell checker doesn't care whether a moose or a mouse is loose in your house.

Additional tip: when checking format and alignments, moving the page view at the bottom of the screen to 60% allows you to see two full pages at a time, which makes it easier to spot rogue indents and line spaces. (Remember to make adjustments from the tool bar).

We have come a long way. At this stage – after proofreading – I print out the corrected manuscript, mock-up a cover with the working title and some artwork, and have it spiral-bound. This boost to morale has been well-earned. Good though it is to see a tangible product of your hard work sitting on your desk, especially as the next stage involves several weeks of patiently waiting for feedback, this is not its only purpose.

During those weeks you will consider the next stage (publishing options), and continue thinking about your book. As ideas come to you, note them in the appropriate section of your hard copy for further thought when you have received and assembled all the review comments.

Feedback and external editing:

Once your manuscript is as complete and accurate as you can make it, you are ready to send it out for feedback. Ideally, this will include comments from one or more pre-readers, or critiquers (also called beta-readers) as well as a professional editor.

Using pre-readers:

An appropriate pre-reader is someone who either comes within your earlier definition of 'readers', or who shares your expertise, or both. The process is informal in that pre-readers are not generally paid: you are asking them for a personal favour and may be able to reciprocate in other ways. Their role is to comment on your work, pointing out positive and negative aspects to give you a reader's response. Friends, colleagues or family members can do this, but the most essential requirement is that they should be frank. If you're lucky, as well as giving you feedback, your pre-readers will be sharp enough to point out errors you have overlooked.

Relatives are often reluctant to give honest opinions for fear of hurting your feelings, but for memoir, and family or local history, their input may be especially valuable.

For a reader to experience the whole book is obviously beneficial to me as a writer, but in addition, if I am concerned about a specific chapter, I ask a person with knowledge in that area to read it.

Ask your pre-readers for written comments, so that you can refer back later, and if they also discuss their views with you, listen carefully, rather than argue to justify what you wrote. Their critique is their opinion – which you asked for – it does not mean you automatically change your manuscript, but that you become aware of additional insights to consider, especially if several people express similar sentiments. Sometimes pre-readers' views are contradictory and you have to assess their relative value.

People take time to read and comment, so send your manuscript to an external editor while waiting for your pre-readers' feedback.

Hiring a professional editor:

A professional editor will analyse the same aspects of your manuscript that you did in your revision, but with a trained eye. Good editors point out errors, make suggestions and give advice: they do not rewrite or add text to anything you have written. If your editor shares knowledge of your subject, that is a bonus. More important – unless the subject is extremely technical or specialised – is that he or she has expertise and experience in editing nonfiction, and returns your manuscript at the agreed time.

For such skilled and detailed work we must pay fees. Copyediting – a line-by-line scrutiny – will cost the most because of the time involved; a general critique – similar to our 'stage one revision' above – will cost less, but you would need to be confident in your language skills to opt only for this.

Where to find a good editor? Word of mouth recommendations are the surest: ask colleagues, writing groups, the local librarian, or your social media contacts. Depending where you live, other valuable listings are in

The Writers' and Artists' Year Book (for the UK), *New Zealand Writer's Handbook*, and the website of the Publishers Association of South Africa, and writing magazines often carry their advertisements. If you search online to find editorial services, check whether they are members of a professional association, or search for 'editor associations + (your country)'.

Most editors operate a website which indicates the genres they work in and their average fees per word count. They should also provide references from clients. Contact a few people who have hired them and ask about their experience. Many editors are also writers – reading some of their work will give you an idea of their standards.

Once you make contact, an editor should be willing to indicate their experience, quote a fee for the service you ask for, and give a firm estimate of the time it will take them to complete the work. Be realistic about time-scales: good editors may be booked up for weeks ahead.

If you want to trial an editor's services before committing your whole manuscript, send one chapter, or the 1,000 word piece you wrote at the beginning, ask for a full edit and see how it works out.

Finalising your manuscript:

Once you have gathered the comments of pre-readers and the feedback from your editor, take time to mull over what you have learned from them and make final revisions to the manuscript. Proofread it all again and, after a week or two, proof it once more.

By this stage, you have created a complete and polished manuscript ready to be submitted to a publisher, or to publish yourself with the confidence that it is the best you can write and is presented to a professional standard.

What to do now:

→   Contact potential pre-readers (ideally, a minimum of two people, if possible) so they are available when you are ready.

→ Identify an external editor to negotiate terms and book dates for working on your project.

→ Carry out the two stages of your own reviewing and revise as required.

→ Proofread and correct the manuscript. Leave it for at least a week and repeat.

→ Send copies of the manuscript (preferably as a Word document for economy) to pre-readers.

→ Send a copy of the manuscript to your editor (a Word document is usual).

→ Read Chapter 8 and start publisher research while waiting for pre-reader and editor responses.

→ When all the feedback is received, complete your final revisions; proofread and correct any errors.

Part Three

Get it Out

8.

Decide the Best
Publishing Option for You

A brief overview of the book industry:

Before deciding which of the publishing options is most suitable for your shiny new manuscript, it would be well to take a brief overview of the book industry and the state of flux in which it now appears to operate. (Because of the problem in defining a moving target, I use 'book industry' as a general term to encompass what happens between a manuscript being completed and a reader reading the book in whatever form).

Traditionally, an author's work passed through the hands of a considerable cast of players:

- Literary agents who screen manuscript submissions and choose which authors to represent and promote to potential publishers.

- Publishers who select which manuscripts to publish, based on the genres they handle and the marketability of the book.

- Printers and designers who produce the physical product.

- Distributors – the wholesalers – who warehouse the books for a specific list of publishers and from whom bookshops and libraries buy their stock centrally.

- Booksellers and libraries who select which books to stock from the titles available to them through the distributors.

- Readers who choose which books to read and/or buy.

This is still the principal model, but significant changes are blurring old boundaries. Roles are not as clear-cut as they were, some members of the cast now speak each other's lines, and new actors are coming on stage still learning their parts. Authors, too, can now become publishers, distributors and retailers of their own, and others', books more easily than in the past. Roles and functions are expanding, becoming more fluid, in some cases, merging.

A number of literary agents now offer fee-based services to authors who wish to self-publish; some have established their own publishing divisions, raising questions about the possible clash of interests in their dealings with an author's query.

Publishing has always involved disparities in company size, but takeovers and mergers in recent years have further concentrated the industry in the hands of a few top players – commonly referred to as the 'Big Six' – while the ease of digital book production has drawn new, small and micro-companies in at lower levels, creating wider disparities. The 2012 merger between Penguin and Random House produced the largest publishing empire in the world and, like the other five conglomerates – Macmillan; Harper Collins; Simon and Schuster; Harlequin, and Hatchette – they own hundreds of imprints world-wide, including most of the household names sitting on your bookshelves.

Some larger companies operate their own warehousing and distribution systems, and many publishers – including four of the 'Big Six' – now incorporate self-publishing divisions, selling to authors a range of services from specific technical assistance to complete publishing packages. Distributors of digital books also sell direct, and an increasing number of publishers of all sizes, act as retailers by selling books from their own online stores.

Printing has seen the development of print on demand (POD), also made possible by digital technology, which makes it economic for a printer to produce small numbers of books at short notice – often within 48 hours. Many small publishers now opt for this system because it saves warehousing costs and reduces losses from unsold stock. It also makes print editions more feasible for self-publishing authors; some POD companies offer a full book design service for self-publishing.

The role of bookselling has also expanded, though less so for small independent bookshops. In the most notable example, from being an online print-book retailer, Amazon has become a global force in almost all aspects of the book industry, not only by selling ebooks, but as a distribution channel for self-published work and, more recently, launching its own publishing imprint. Other major bookstores have also created a strong retail presence online for both print and ebooks.

And new players have emerged. Both Kobo and Apple (who began as technology developers) matched their production of digital reading devices with distribution services for self-published authors; they are also significant retailers of digital books. Such pressure from online retailing of both print and digital books has caused some high street booksellers to close their stores.

Even the reading experience has new dimensions. Definitions of 'book' and the process of reading continue to metamorphose into ever varied forms on multiple media. From cell phones to tablets, new reading devices offer massive choice to customers. Despite attempts to prevent piracy, an increasingly techno-savvy public find ways around controls. Sites offering thousands of discounted and free ebooks – legally and illegally – have created new expectations among many readers that books should be cheap, and preferably free.

The reasons for all this turbulence are complex, but digital technology, which continues to open up new approaches to production, marketing and reading, accounts for much of it, along with attendant economic pressures as publishers and retailers jostle to retain their share of the market.

How do these shifts affect you with a manuscript ready for publication?

- Opinions differ as to whether it is becoming more difficult to be accepted by literary agents and mainstream publishers. It has always been harder for unknown, first-time authors, and more people seem to write and seek publication now than ever before. But 'everyone' seems to be writing novels, competition is less for nonfiction works and the chances of publication are better, especially if you identify the right market and target an appropriate publisher.

- In the 'traditional model' for nonfiction, a literary agent approaches a publisher, on an author's behalf, with a proposal and sample chapters; if accepted, the author is paid an advance and writes the book. This system saves authors from completing a book that turns out to be unsuitable for the market. However, an increasing number of publishers will not consider a proposal from an unknown author unless a full manuscript is available, if they should ask for it. This is why I emphasised the importance of market research at the beginning: your manuscript should aim at an identified slot in the market to increase its chances of acceptance.

- Presumably as a result of financial pressures, many publishers now provide less editing support than previously, as a result, a manuscript that has already been professionally edited and polished is a more attractive investment to a publisher.

- Another outcome of reduced operating budgets is that, whether authors are published by one of the 'Big Six', by a micro publisher, or are publishing their work themselves, they are required to participate in promoting and marketing their books: it has become part of an author's role, and is the main reason for establishing an author platform.

- The entry of new publishing companies into the industry, especially the smaller ones and those specialising in digital production, has increased the opportunities for first-time authors to be published. Advances may be minimal, or non-existent, but these outlets can provide an important first step into publication and are worth pursuing.

- For authors who want to self-publish, the technology has never been more accessible, or the costs less. Whether carrying out all the work yourself, or hiring technical expertise for part, or all, of the procedure, it has never been easier to publish a book – selling it is a different matter. Because of the sheer volume of new print and digital books coming onto the market every week, being 'discovered' – having your title seen by potential purchasers – is the biggest challenge, and why effective marketing is vital.

- It has never been easier, or cheaper, to privately print and distribute books, whether as gifts, as presentations, or to sell direct to the public, perhaps as a fund-raiser, or to recover the costs of a book produced principally for other purposes.

- The fastest growing sector in the book industry is self-publishing. Agents, publishers, printers and online distributors are tapping into this new business opportunity by offering services to self-publishing authors. In the environment of merging and blurring roles already described, it becomes hard at times to know exactly who you are dealing with – we will discuss ways of identifying different services, but it is essentially a case of buyer beware.

- Finally, it should be clear by now that any modern author who wishes to be published, must play a role in the market-place, and needs to understand as much as possible about its operations. Only with such knowledge can you gain advantages and avoid pitfalls.

Overall, authors now have increased responsibilities however they publish, but new opportunities also create more choice. What is available to you locally will depend on which country you live in, but publishing is a global enterprise, so consider widening your search to find possibilities elsewhere when making your publishing decision.

What are your main options?

Attempting to define the range of publishing prospects that would apply in all countries would be impossibly complex. Even definitions are problematic because of shifting roles and functions: If a publisher offers a traditional contract to one author, but asks another to pay for a publishing package (i.e. vanity publishing), is it still a 'traditional publisher'? Is being published by a vanity publisher the same as being self-published, or is that only if you do it all yourself? And what exactly is an 'indie author'?

Thinking about this, I realised that the simplest, clearest approach to help you find your way through all of this and decide what to do next, is to focus on you as the author and the role you want to play – to give you the tools to work out for yourself the solution that best fits your purpose and your topic. You have created an original work, this is what you start with, and there are three main roles you can adopt in getting it out into the market – as a buyer, a seller, or an entrepreneur:

Buy a publishing package –

You could buy a complete publishing package from a vanity publisher (also called 'fully assisted', or 'subsidy' publishing): you pay the full costs of publishing as well as assign the publishing rights, and receive a royalty payment from sales. No agent is required and, as preparation of the manuscript for publication is often minimal, the process is usually quicker than the traditional route. As you are the only party investing in the book, you have the greater interest in the quality of the final product, but you will have little control over it.

Sell the publishing rights –

You could sell the rights to publish your manuscript to a publisher willing to invest in your book (i.e. by making a submission – the 'traditional route'): a publisher takes the financial risks and pays you royalties (usually around 7%-10%) based on the book's sales revenue. Most large publishers require you to have a literary agent, but both publisher and agent receive their income from your book sales: you pay neither of them directly.

The whole process from seeking an agent to having your book for sale can take 2-3 years, or longer. Many small publishers do not require you to have an agent and the process is quicker, even more so with a specialist digital publisher (who is also likely to pay a higher royalty).

Self-publish as an entrepreneur –

You could adopt an entrepreneurial role in self-publishing your book: you can hire technical or professional assistance as required for any part of the process, but you retain the full publishing rights yourself as the publisher, and you exercise control over the whole procedure. You also retain all the revenue from book sales – less retailers' and distributors' fees. This is the quickest publishing method, depending on the time you spend preparing for publication, and the turn-around time of any specialist services you hire. But it does not mean that establishing sales and an author reputation is equally quick: successful publishing is a long-term business whichever process you employ.

All three options apply to both print and digital publishing: most traditional publishers issue digital editions of their books and, (for an additional fee), a vanity publisher will do the same. And remember that the 'rights' referred to above are rights to publish your work, (usually exclusive to the publisher concerned and for an agreed period), *not* the copyright which is always yours, (although a copyright *can* be sold, it is rarely, if ever, in an author's interests to do so).

From what we have discussed so far in this chapter, you will probably not be surprised to learn that there are variations and hybrid arrangements in the three options I have outlined, but if you focus on who is making the most investment (and has the highest motivation for sales success), and who holds the publishing rights (and therefore control for the duration of the contract), you will have a clearer idea of your real costs and potential benefits as you investigate each publishing opportunity – and you should do so carefully.

Your next step is to decide which role you wish to play, and to help you to do that, the remainder of this chapter explains more fully what is involved in each option and how each can be achieved.

Buying a full publishing package:

Vanity publishing acquired its name in the days when it offered the only means for eccentric aunts and retired colonels to publish their memoirs, however tedious the reading – the single consideration being the sizeable funds required. They could have had their musings simply type-set and printed, distributing the books themselves as many 19th century writers did, but this lacks the prestige of having a publisher's imprint on the title page.

As a result of this reputation, one of the problems with vanity publishers, for an author, is that bookshops rarely stock their books and mainstream media do not review them, so they are extremely difficult to market.

The reason for this is not solely snobbery; it reflects also the fact that vanity publishers have little vested interest in the quality of a book. They receive their money at the outset with no risk, regardless of whether any copies are sold; unlike traditional publishers, whose livelihood depends on sales, and who have to pay editors, proof-readers, designers, printers, publicists and an author's advance before they sell a single volume. A tiny fraction of submissions to mainstream publishers are accepted for publication.

However, the reasons for traditional publishers rejecting a manuscript vary widely: it doesn't mean it is not worthy of publication. If you have followed the steps in this book, hired an external editor and completed your revisions, you will know this. It is difficult for unknown, first-time authors to be taken on by agents, or to be accepted by large publishers, and it takes time and research to find the right smaller publisher who will accept a direct submission.

In this situation, vanity publishing might seem an attractive option without the hassle and technological knowledge required for publishing yourself. But you should be aware that, although some companies offer a useful range of services, others are an expensive rip-off, providing little more than promises. So if you wish to pursue this option, you should check each one carefully.

Because they don't call themselves 'vanity publishers' it is sometimes difficult to know, from an initial cruise around their website, that this is what they are. They list submission guidelines and talk about the genres they handle as many publishers do, but somewhere else on the site will be their price package, usually a range from 'economy' to 'premium'. There might also be a reading fee for assessing your manuscript.

The terminology varies: some companies describe themselves as traditional publishers offering 'traditional partnership', 'contributory publication', or 'contribution-based contracts' as alternatives. They indicate that the submission process is the same for all authors: only when you receive that longed-for 'acceptance letter' are you told that you must pay a large sum of money to make it happen.

And as the process unfolds, there may be no editing, no proofreading, no advice or support, resulting in a poor quality product with no marketing – unless you make a further payment for a 'marketing package'. In attempting to avoid a perceived stigma as 'self-published' by having a named publisher, their clients acquire the stigma of 'vanity author', an added difficulty in building an author platform to promote the book.

Clients of vanity publishers may pay several thousand dollars to have a manuscript processed for listing on Amazon, for anyone who might be able to find it, and that is all – a service that is readily available from experts for a couple of hundred dollars. A sound company should be open about their role and the costs involved, and list authors and titles so that you can contact those who have been published by them. Access some of their books in online stores; read the marketing blurb and the covers to see how good they are; look to see what other marketing they do for their authors – profile pages on their website for example.

Search the company name online and see what write-ups emerge. Web addresses for three useful sites – Preditors and Editors, Writer Beware, and the Publishing Services Index – are given in the Appendices.

If you decide to go ahead, ask a legal professional to check the contract, (if there is a society or association of authors in your area, they may offer this service, or suggest someone who does). You will be assigning the exclusive rights to publish your work – a process you pay for in full – in exchange for a royalty on sales. For how long do they hold these rights? For how long do they guarantee the book will be in print and/or digital form and available? Is the royalty calculated on gross sale price of the book or on net price (i.e. after the publisher deducts further expenses)?

And check the procedure for ending the contract if you wish to do so. If the company fails to market or distribute your book effectively, it could be tied up uselessly for years, preventing you from publishing in any other way. Authors with a traditional mainstream publisher can still find themselves neglected at the bottom of the publisher's list, with no marketing budget for their books, but at least they have not paid thousands of dollars for the privilege.

Some companies offering 'author services' blur the line between vanity publishing and self-publishing. This is why I make the distinction between assigning any publishing rights (vanity publishing), and retaining all rights yourself (self-publishing), to make it easier for you to differentiate them and make your preferred choice.

Author Solutions is one of the largest suppliers of author services and provides an interesting example of the creeping integration within publishing that makes it hard for writers or readers to know who they are dealing with. Author Solutions offers a range of assistance packages from writing through to marketing, and uses several different imprints for the books it publishes for its clients; part of its allure for authors is the listing under a publishing imprint which draws a veil over the vanity aspect.

The 'veil' was glamorised in July 2012 when the company was bought by Penguin (now Penguin Random House). Since then, (despite online criticism of Author Solutions' business dealings and a current legal case against it), Author Solutions has been engaged to operate the self-publishing imprints of three other 'Big Six' publishing houses: Simon and Schuster, Harlequin, and Harper Collins.

Submitting to traditional publishers:

As I mentioned earlier, most large publishing houses only accept submissions from authors through a literary agent. Aiming at this target is the longest route to publication and the hardest, because only a small percentage of authors achieve a publishing deal with major companies. On the other hand, thousands of authors worldwide *are* published by mainstream publishers each year: with the right book and a dose of luck, you could be one of them.

In general, the smaller the publisher, the more likely they are to accept direct submissions, and more publishers appear to be doing so. In countries where a publishing industry is still emerging, or where traditions have developed differently, there may be few, if any, literary agents. In this situation, local publishers generally consider direct submissions, although the number of books they issue each year may be small. Whatever the size of publisher, with a traditional route, a print book will be distributed to bookshops, and the book stands a better chance of being reviewed by mainstream media which is important to any book's sales success.

This section covers working with, and without, an agent, and finding publishers of all sizes, including micro companies and those specialising in digital production.

Many publishers include nonfiction works as part of a wider list of other genres, but some specialise in nonfiction and these are often a good place to start. Promising possibilities to consider are:

- academic presses attached to universities: these can cover almost any subject, but establishing your credibility and expertise is especially important

- institutions and organisations promoting particular issues: e.g. the environment, health, parenting, business development

- niche publishers specialising in particular subjects: e.g. illustrated guides, sport, national and military histories, museums, music and the arts

- publishers with a strong regional focus: a publisher based in your region may be interested in a local author's memoir, or in books about the area's history, geography, food, and so on

- small presses specialising in ethnic and cultural issues, or publishing authors with relevant ethnic affiliations: present in many countries, including New Zealand, Australia, South Africa, Canada, and the USA

- micro companies (new as well as well-established publishers): because of their flexibility, they are often innovative, even experimental; they may produce fewer titles each year than their larger competitors, but they can provide the first important step into publication

- publishers specialising in digital publication: for a topical subject, e.g. dealing with an urgent current issue, a small digital publisher is the quickest way to have a book on the market in a traditional deal.

Additional advantages of digital publishing over print are that your book remains available as long as you and the publisher choose to have it online – as it takes up no shelf-room like a physical book, it is not moved out ('remaindered') to make way for new releases – and it can be distributed globally within days, without the complex procedures of negotiating territorial rights required for traditional print publication.

Whichever type of traditional publishing you aim for, you need a great idea and a unique approach: exceptional content and a well-written and polished manuscript will give you the best possible chance of publishing success. But it is essential to target publishers that work with your genre. To find them, there is no alternative to spending time on research.

Searching for nonfiction publishers and agents:

Although *The Writers & Artists Year Book* lists mainly publishers in the UK, it is worth remembering that many of these companies work with authors world-wide, or have subsidiary offices in other countries. The list includes a wide range of publishers, but not all the smaller companies that can open the door for first-time authors. The Internet will find those if you filter your search and check individual sites.

If you simply search for 'nonfiction publishers' you'll be inundated with a mix of results including self-publishing and vanity presses. It is best to start with data bases or directories and work from there. The following are sites with listings of nonfiction publishers alphabetically, by country and/or by topic. Some also quote a brief company description:

- http://www.writewords.org.uk/directory/
- www.bookdoctor.com.au/nonfiction.html (an Australian site)
- http://www.publishsa.co.za/members-and-freelancers/members/publishers/list (List of nonfiction publishers who are members of the South African Publishers Association)
- www.publishersglobal.com

It will save time and frustration if you plan your research. Find which of these directories is most helpful to you and select an initial list of a dozen likely publishers – save their websites on your 'favourites' – and then access each site checking out the following:

- Are they regular publishers, or self-publishing/author services sites?

- Do they publish your genre of nonfiction?

- Find the 'submissions' page (sometimes this information is on the 'contact page'): do they work directly with authors or only through agents?

- Check if guidelines are different for fiction/nonfiction – they might accept direct nonfiction submissions.

- How long do they take to assess a submission (most give some guidance)?

- Do they state 'exclusive submissions only' – i.e. you can't submit to others at the same time? (Non-exclusive submissions save you a lot of waiting time).

- Look at their titles: are they appealing to the same readership that you are aiming for?

- Look at the 'about' page: is there any special feature that makes you or your book a good match for them?

You may have to repeat this exercise a few times to accumulate a working list of the most appropriate publishers that suit your purpose. You can find out more about each of your 'possibles' by entering their names in a Wikipedia search, and if you have any doubts, on the Writers Beware, and Editors and Preditors data bases.

Finding an agent follows the same procedure. There are fewer of them, which makes the task easier. If necessary, extend the field with an online search for 'directory of literary agents' which produces a list of directories, including some of those mentioned above for publishers. There might also be an association of agents in your country which provides a list of members. In addition, writing and publishing magazines often carry features by agents, or issue news of book releases which mention the agent, and authors on social media often state in their profiles who represents them (or would be willing to tell you if asked).

Not all agents handle all genres, nor are they all open to taking on new clients, so follow the same research plan as for publishers to create a list of possibilities.

Unless you have already decided with which level of publisher to begin your submission process, it is advisable to keep all your options open for as long as possible. The following strategy will enable you to do that.

- Finding an agent to represent you takes many months, so send query letters to agents at the same time as you send submissions to publishers. If a publisher accepts you in the meantime, decide whether to go ahead (without an agent), or continue agent-hunting: with a publisher's acceptance already, you are a good prospect for an agent.

- Submit to multiple publishers who do not say your submission should be 'exclusive.'

- If submitting to one at a time, send first to those quoting the shortest time for consideration: some may take 6 weeks; others, 6 months. Small and micro publishers are likely to respond more quickly, but almost everyone takes longer than they say.

- Edit your submission to make your approach specific to each publisher or agent.

- Study each publisher's 'submission guidelines' for *nonfiction* carefully and send exactly what they ask for in the form specified. The same applies for querying agents.

- Some publishers accept submissions only at certain times of the year: abide by this or your time and effort will be wasted.

How do you make submissions to agents and publishers? I explain querying and working with agents in the next section, but first, we'll see what is involved in making a direct submission to a publisher of any category.

Making direct submissions to publishers:

From our brief review of the book industry you will realise that, like any other business, publishers operate to make a profit. When approaching them, be aware of their point of view: new authors are a financial risk – their skills and the potential marketability of their work is an 'unknown'. And some publishers receive over 200 submissions a week. But like all businesses, they are constantly on the lookout for the next 'great idea' – it could be yours.

Your submission is your sales pitch. The main objectives are to stand out from the mass and to alleviate the 'unknown' aspect. Not by writing on fluorescent paper in an obscure font, nor by saying 'this is the most fantastic book you will read this year', but by providing clear, concise, accurate information that shows a publisher you have thought about their needs and the readers they cater for, and that you have something special to offer them. In addition to providing information, your submission should demonstrate your writing skills sufficiently to make them want to read the manuscript.

In their 'submission guidelines', publishers usually ask for a covering letter (a few issue a pro-forma instead); a proposal (which includes an outline of chapters), and one or more complete sample chapters. Publishers that only consider a submission after the whole manuscript is complete are likely to ask for a one-page synopsis instead of a proposal. The next section describes how to write each of these.

Writing a covering letter:

The covering letter is the first (and possibly only) part of your submission the publisher's editor will read. It should fit onto *one side* of an A4 page (single spaced in 12pt standard font such as Times New Roman) and include:

- The title and focus of the work and how it is unique (grab their interest at the start)

- The readership likely to buy it and why, e.g. a need and how your book fills it

- Whether the work is illustrated, e.g. graphs, photographs, other art work

- Why you are particularly qualified to write on this subject

- Any market advantage you possess (e.g. a college, organisation, travel company etc is already interested in using your work, or mention media coverage your activities have attracted)

Edit your first draft until you have constructed four or five concise paragraphs in perfect grammar. Allowing for addresses, greeting and signing off, there will be room for little more than 200 words in total in the body of your letter. You will want to say more about some items than others, so prioritise your strongest points. Use the same structure whether they ask for an email or a hard-copy letter, adding your email address to both; if you run a website, quote the web address at the bottom of the page.

Address the letter personally to the commissioning editor with their

142

full name ('Dear Jonathan Clark'), correctly spelled – e.g. is there an 'e' in 'Clarke'? Publishing people are touchy about such things. More importantly, an error shows lack of attention to accuracy and detail: not a good image for a nonfiction writer.

Compiling a proposal and outline:

The proposal gives you the opportunity to enlarge on items mentioned in the covering letter with some supporting facts and figures, where appropriate.

Begin with a 'title page' quoting the title of your manuscript, the genre, the word count, your name and full contact details and the date of submission. On the next page, in double spacing and in concise, clear paragraphs, expand on the key points of your pitch.

The unique feature of your work might include new data; an experience no one else has had; a country few have visited; an easy introduction to a difficult subject; an innovative way of doing something, or a humorous look at an unexpected topic. Explain how you handle this in the manuscript and the tone in which it is written.

When describing your target audience, identify them numerically if possible, e.g. for a book aimed at students, how many are enrolled in the subject? Define what need the book fulfils, and the reasons readers would buy it, for example, in a recession, small companies are especially under pressure, if your book details ways to increase profitability in a particular sector, it could help your readers stay in business. Quote an authoritative estimate of how many such companies are operating.

If there are no books like yours – i.e. your research found a genuine gap in the market – this is a good selling point (provided you can show there is a potential market for it). If there are other competing titles, mention a couple of them and explain how yours is better, e.g. more up to date; more accessible approach; different angle. Be diplomatic: focus on what you offer, not on criticising another author – she might be the editor's wife or daughter.

Include a section on marketing possibilities you can provide: trade or professional connections that would increase awareness; potential or past media coverage; your social media activities and any ways in which you can personally boost promotion. Consider timing of public events that would draw attention to your book – in the last couple of years we've celebrated Charles Darwin's 150th anniversary, the World Cup, the London Olympics, and the 50th anniversary of the *Dr Who* series, all marked by new nonfiction books and creating promotional opportunities for other related titles.

Demonstrated expertise is essential in nonfiction works. If you are writing about food, your particular knowledge might stem from being a chef, running a restaurant or operating a market garden. You may experience health or personal issues that uniquely qualify you to write how-to or self-help advice in dealing with them. These can be mentioned briefly as part of defining the value or uniqueness of your material, but should also be covered in more detail in an author biography ('bio').

An author biography is much more selective than a CV. Write it in the third person and quote specific information that provides credibility for your subject expertise and writing skills. Include only what relates directly to your submission, for example, relevant qualifications and experience; professional memberships; activities in local or national interest groups; awards; previous publications and other writing.

The second part of your proposal is the outline. Starting with the chapter outline you constructed at the beginning as a basis, pare each chapter summary down to about five lines (approximately 100 words) that convey the essence of each chapter. Read it through and edit again to ensure that the logical progression from one chapter to the next is still clear. And, as far as possible, write in the same style as in your manuscript.

The publisher may specify which chapter/s they want to read, e.g. the first only, or the first and second. If no specification is given, you can choose what you believe to be the best, but don't send more chapters than they ask for.

The total length of your proposal will depend on what the submission guidelines indicate. Some specify no more than 10 pages in total for the complete submission. If it is unclear whether or not the total pages include sample chapters, contact the company to ask, (either the guidelines or the 'contact us' page on the website should say whether they prefer telephone or email enquiries).

Writing a synopsis:

Many publishers now ask only for a one-page, or a 300-word, synopsis and a sample chapter in an initial submission, along with a covering, or 'introductory' letter.

The synopsis is not simply a summary of the book; neither does it describe the book. I think of it as a miniature experience of the manuscript, a bit like a film or video trailer which portrays atmosphere, tone and high spots. It is written in the 'third person' ('Mike Blogs canoed the rapids…' not 'I canoed the rapids…') and has to achieve several things:

- Excite the reader from the very first line
- Show the logic of the whole narrative from its starting point to the conclusion
- Highlight essential features with a mix of general principles and interesting details
- Demonstrate your writing style and overall treatment of the subject

Time spent on a synopsis is a good investment because it also forms the basis for future cover blurbs, press releases and other promotion. Such a low word count is challenging, but this page can be written in single spacing. As a starting point, pare down your earlier chapter outline as described above, so you can appreciate the essence of the whole narrative in a potted form, and think about your readers: How do you want them to respond to your book? What do you want them to feel or do? With this in mind, write your synopsis as a mini-experience for them. Review and edit, try it out on a few people, and stay within the word count.

Illustrations:

Publishers who deal with illustrated books will state in their submission guidelines whether you can send images and in what form. If sending photographs, select only the very best, and, if sending by email, remember to re-size them as jpeg images. If you keep image files in online 'cloud storage' facilities, you may be able to make high resolution images accessible to others if they are registered in the same system.

For a hard-copy submission, send a DVD or a selection of prints – whatever the guidelines specify. If pictures are important to your book and they are not mentioned in the guidelines, contact the company to ask if you can send illustrations and in what form. Send copies, not originals. Don't send too many: two or three stunning images deliver greater impact and remain more memorable than the visual overload of fifteen.

Assembling the complete submission –

- Re-read the submission guidelines to make sure you have assembled everything required, and check whether they want it by email or by post (with return postage).

- For all pages making up the submission, use a standard font such as Times New Roman in 12 point on A4 page size; number all the pages consecutively; insert a 'header' with your name, book title and email address on each page.

- For hard-copy submissions, make sure the printing is clean and secure with clips not staples.

- Keep a copy of everything – there is no guarantee it will be returned, even if you enclosed a stamped addressed envelope for this purpose.

- Double check name spellings and proofread everything a dozen times because the stress of sending out a submission affects our efficiency. Leave for a day and re-check everything again before sending.

- When it has gone, relax and give yourself a treat.

When a publisher asks to read your complete manuscript, send exactly what they ask for by the method specified. To avoid your work being mistaken on arrival for an 'unsolicited manuscript' and possibly being consigned to the bin, write on the outside of the envelope, (or in the subject line of the email), 'Requested Material'.

Reading your publishing contract –

Most authors go through the submission process many times and it becomes easier with practise. If a publisher's interest is roused, they will ask to see the whole manuscript and you wait, again, while that is considered. But one day, an acceptance letter arrives and corks are popped.

But read the contract in a sober frame of mind. It should specify not only royalty rates and a publication date, but what rights you are assigning. Copyright is always yours as the creator of the material, but publishing rights are complex. They may include rights to publish in other countries, i.e. foreign rights; translations; audio books and digital editions. You should ensure you are fairly compensated for your work in all these different forms. I strongly recommend you obtain professional advice so that you understand exactly what is involved before you sign. *The Writers and Artists Year Book* gives general advice on contracts and lists firms who deal with them, but you may need to find someone in your own country who can give this advice.

Submitting through a literary agent –

The role of an agent is to represent authors to potential publishers; deal with the business aspects of negotiating contracts and publishing rights; handle finances, and in some cases, work with authors and publishers on marketing and promotion. Fees range from 10% – 17% of the royalties a book earns. An agent's income depends on how your book sells; your success is their success and that is a good incentive system. For this reason, it is unwise to engage an agent who asks for fees in advance to read your manuscript, or for any other purpose.

I described earlier in this chapter how to find agents and make a list of possibilities. Agents vary widely in their genres preferences, their style of working and the degree of support and extent of communication with individual authors. As well as checking whether they accept your genre and topic of nonfiction, it is wise to do some homework on how the agent operates: being tied to a 'partner' who turns out to be incompatible is worse than having no agent at all. An agent's website usually lists who they represent and indicates how many clients are on their books, and may include other information about how they work. Personal attention is likely to be less in a large set-up where an agent handles many clients.

Once you have identified suitable agents, check submission guidelines on how to approach them – called 'querying' – and follow their instructions. If there is no guidance, send only a 'query letter' initially. Address each agent by name (yes, double check the spelling), say why you seek representation from that agency, and construct a short concise letter like the 'covering letter' for publishers.

More than one agent may respond to your query by asking for a proposal, a synopsis or a sample chapter. You should submit these to only one agent at a time, so choose which one best fits your work and send them exactly what they ask for, stating that you are submitting to them exclusively. As agents receive many unsolicited manuscripts which are binned or destroyed, avoid the shredder by writing 'Requested material' on the outside of the envelope or in the subject line of an email. Expect to wait six or eight weeks for a reply (you are unlikely to receive an acknowledgement). If you hear nothing, and a follow-up letter after that period receives no response, repeat the procedure with the next agent on your list.

If you are offered representation, ask them what will happen once you sign up with them. What are their terms? Do they charge administration or any other fees in addition to a percentage of royalties? What is the duration of the agreement – a set period or indefinite? (An agent's contract can extend beyond the life of the author and entail claims on his or her literary estate).

Other questions to consider are whether the agreement includes *all* your writing? For example, if you sell freelance articles through your own efforts, would the agent expect to receive a percentage of these earnings? And what are the arrangements for ending the contract by either side? If an agent is unwilling to answer any of these questions, or is annoyed by them, it should start you wondering whether this would be a good working relationship for you.

It can be a frustratingly long process, which is why I suggest the strategy above of approaching, at the same time, publishers who accept direct submissions. Another method you can employ, a route that has opened up as a result of recent changes in the publishing industry and the difficulty first-time authors experience in breaking into traditional publication, is to engage a literary consultant.

The role of literary consultants:

Literary consultancies read and assess your manuscript, send you a detailed report on its strengths and weaknesses, and advise on its marketability and the most suitable publishing route. Editing or other services for preparing manuscripts may also be available. They do not publish books, but if they regard your manuscript as ready for submission, and likely to be accepted, they recommend it to agents with whom they are in contact. Their assessors – 'readers' – have experience in publishing, either as authors, agents, or in some other capacity, and these relationships may be helpful in finding an agent to represent you.

Fees are about the same as for an editor and vary according to the length of manuscript, so ask for quotes and make some comparisons. You may consider that the report and advice you receive is worth the cost, especially if they decide to recommend your manuscript, but there is no guarantee that they will find you an agent, or a publisher.

Search for literary consultants in the same places as for agents; check their websites and ask for references or clients you can contact. Also look for any official recognition: some are recommended by national arts councils, authors' associations or other major institutions.

Whatever your chosen route: maximise your chances of success with a well-prepared manuscript and an irresistible synopsis or proposal, targeted at the most appropriate publisher or agent for your specific topic.

Dealing with Rejections:

Rejections are inevitable, everyone receives them. They are almost a badge of membership for writers who pursue the long-haul route of seeking a traditional deal with a large publisher.

Reasons for rejection are numerous and may reflect what suits a publisher at a particular time, rather than the quality of your work – it does not mean that your manuscript is not good enough for publication. But if you receive any comments, however brief, in a rejection letter from an agent or a publisher, study them carefully because they may indicate ways to strengthen your submissions, or adjust your manuscript to improve its marketability.

The term used in publishing is 'submitting' and at times it does seem a masochistic experience. Success requires patience and persistence. If this represents too long a time-scale for you, or you prefer to remain entirely independent and publish your own work, we look at that option next.

Self-publishing Your Book:

I have defined 'self-publishing' as the option in which you retain your publishing rights and exercise control over the whole process. Depending on your goal, this may involve releasing your book onto the open market to gain maximum exposure and sales, or printing and distributing it privately if it is, for example, a family history, a promotional tool for your business, or a fund-raiser for a local cause. We look at the open-market process first, because several aspects of that are also helpful for private publishing.

Self-publishing is not necessarily the easiest option and there are in-built limitations on the market exposure your book is likely to receive, but it is the choice many first-time authors make, especially for digital books which account for a larger share of the book trade each year.

As a self-published author (what is usually meant by 'indie author'), *you* are the publisher, with the right to control the whole process. That right brings with it the responsibility for book and cover design, issuing the book through distributors/retailers, marketing and promotion, customer relations and everything else involved in the business of producing, publishing and selling a book – you become an entrepreneur.

But you don't have to implement all of this yourself; professional assistance geared to indie publications is readily available, and not only through expensive, revenue-collecting author services. If you already have relevant skills you can apply, e.g. graphic art or computer wizardry, you can access software programmes and advisory services for help and support. Like any other publisher, you will gather a team around you to inject various inputs and the choice of that team is critical.

In an earlier section, I pointed out how the boundaries between vanity publishing and self-publishing are often blurred by providers of 'author services'. It is important to differentiate between vanity publishers and companies offering genuine services to help authors self-publish their work; these might include any one of editing, cover design, layout and printing, digital conversion (formatting), marketing, or any combination. Obviously it is necessary to research their websites and talk to their representatives and, if possible, to past clients, but the main characteristics to look for in a genuine self-publishing service are the following:

- Often listed under 'self-publishing services' but always check them.
- Open about assisting self-publishing and displaying costs of each service (these vary so compare prices).
- The author does not assign any publishing rights to the company.
- The company charges a fee for each service provided and does not retain revenue from sales of the book.
- Service provision and payment is a complete procedure – no further strings attached.
- Some companies advertising 'self-publishing support' charge no fee for services and take commission on sales instead, but examine carefully the terms of the contract: Are you signing away any rights?

The most often quoted advantages of self-publishing are that you can display a book on a retailer's site within days, and the services of main distribution channels who lead you through the publishing process, like CreateSpace, Smashwords and Amazon, are inexpensive – some are free.

Speed is an advantage if your book is topical or breaking news and you want it on the market quickly, especially with an ebook that can be downloaded instantly. But quick and cheap are potential traps as much as they are opportunities. Careful preparation and checking at every stage of the process are essential to ensure a quality presentation that can compete against professionals.

A whole book would be needed to explain all the ins and outs of self-publishing, so here, I list only the main tasks and explain briefly what is involved in each.

The basic process of finalising and publishing your manuscript:

- Proofread the manuscript – preferably by a professional, but as a minimum, it should be checked several times by more than one person.
- Compile an Index if required.
- Acquire an ISBN (International Standard Book Number).
- Convert your document file to formats that retailers can accept and resell for customers' reading devices, and that POD providers can use for printing.
- Create a book cover.
- Write a 'product description' – 'blurb' – for retail sites and for a print book cover.
- Upload your book to distribution/retail channels.
- Promote and market your book (covered in the next chapter).

Compiling an index:

An index is usually provided only in a print edition: an ebook can have an expanded Table of Contents (ToC) which is hyperlinked to the text.

It is possible to compile your own index: Microsoft Word includes a programme for this (in the toolbar under 'References') – but it is time-consuming and quite tricky. If it is essential (and it is a mark of quality in a nonfiction print book), it would be worth investigating professional indexing services from reputable writers' resources sites and asking for quotes. Different levels of detail will influence the price: a straight listing of main topics as opposed to cross referencing and sub-topics.

Website addresses are given in the Appendices to societies of indexers in the UK, USA, and Australia/New Zealand which give advice on constructing your own index as well as listing professional services and how to commission them.

Acquiring an ISBN:

The ISBN is the unique numerical identity for each edition of a book, (included on the title page, and also on the back cover of print books) and is required for a book to be distributed and sold commercially. The system is coordinated by the International ISBN Agency, but individual ISBN's are issued by a specified national agency in each country, (see Useful Websites and Books in the Appendices for a link to a list of countries and their agencies).

Creating a cover design:

Unless you are a graphic artist, I strongly recommend you hire a professional cover-design service. Your book cover is the first thing a potential reader sees. The one-second glance of a browsing customer determines whether they pick it up (or click online), or pass by. In that fleeting moment, your cover must attract their attention, show them what the book is about, and motivate them to investigate it further. Look at book covers online and on cover-design websites and notice how different they are for fiction and nonfiction books. The chief requirements for nonfiction cover designs are:

- A title and subtitle clearly indicating the book's contents in as few words as possible – think 'newspaper headlines'. It can be clever – include a pun, for example – but obscure allusions do not attract nonfiction readers. They want to learn or gain something: appeal to the intellect, not the emotions (except perhaps for a memoir).

- Words in the title and subtitle that relate to online retailers' search words for that genre and topic category: 'searchability' leads to 'discovery'.

- Bright primary colours (or none: white has impact) with large clear fonts: the cover must be readable from the thumb–nail sized picture that appears online.

- Artwork that describes the book's contents: for travel, histories, memoirs and biographies, a cameo portrait or scene may be instantly informative of place and period.

- Simple, uncluttered images which leave plenty of surrounding space, or well placed fonts without an image. The aim is not a pretty cover, but one that informs with immediate impact.

Specific considerations for print covers:

- The scope is wider for a print book displayed in a physical bookshop because customers see it in full scale. A cover designed for an ebook can work well in print, but not always the other way round.

- A print book cover should show a short descriptive blurb and author bio on the back, and, if possible, a brief 'review' quote (from a beta reader for example), or endorsement from a credible person in your field. Allow sufficient space (approximately 4cms) at the bottom for a bar code and the ISBN.

- The barcode on print books is simply the ISBN and other information, e.g. price, in a form that can be scanned electronically and may not be necessary in some countries.

Writing a blurb:

The blurb – for the online 'product description', or on the back of a paperback – is one of the most important pieces of text you will write, and will be redrafted and polished many times before you get it right. After the cover, the blurb is the next chance of grabbing the reader's attention. Even then, they may read only the first couple of lines. It all seems grossly unfair that after the effort you have put into writing a book, you are granted only a few seconds of a potential reader's time to convince him or her to buy it, but that is the reality. So here are the key points to remember:

- The blurb should be 200-250 words: if it is longer, it will not fit on the back of a print cover, or in the display space allotted by online distributors – readers would be obliged to click 'more' to read the rest, and they probably won't.

- Don't try to summarise the book: pick its unique aspects and what the reader will learn or gain from reading it.

- The book's chief attractions should be in the first line. What these are depends on the subject of your book, and whether the 'specialness' is in the author, the content, or the readers' potential gain.

Here are some examples of opening phrases: 'Grandmother, Lucy Walsh crossed the Atlantic…'; 'All you need to know about…'; 'Increase your energy. David Blanks unique…'; 'The first published account of…'; 'Grace Mitchell's story of courage, survival and hope…'

- Avoid too much hype and elaborate 'awesome' adjectives because people won't believe it.

- Engage your imagination. Think like a reader: it's your subject, what would make *you* want to buy it?

- Cut, cut and cut again to eliminate every unnecessary word. Write in short and medium-length sentences and spend time perfecting them.

To start you in the right mind-set, here is an example of the opening sentences of a blurb before and after revision:

Initial draft: 'In 2001, Ann Strop left the modern conveniences of her flat in Manchester to travel across the world to Sarawak as a volunteer worker on a community project. She had to cope with unexpected house companions like snakes and bats, as well as all the challenges of understanding a totally different culture. It led to her questioning many of her preconceived ideas on life.'

Revision: 'Snakes in her slippers and bats in the bathroom were the least of Ann Strop's problems. Her adventures as a volunteer in the wilds of Sarawak challenged her outlook on life.'

Converting file formats:

- Your manuscript document has to be converted to one or more main format types: for ebooks – EPUB, and MOBI; for print – PDF.

- Conversions not only enable your book to be printed and/or read on digital devices, they also determine the whole look of the book – margins, page numbering, headings, fonts – and all other book design elements.

- Tables, columns, graphics, boxes and numbered bullet points within your text can cause problems in formatting ebooks, because readers can adjust font size on their reading devices and this disrupts layout.

- If you don't feel confident to do the formatting yourself, conversion/formatting services are available online at reasonable cost.

- Most distribution channels offer file conversion for an additional fee, some are free, and CreateSpace offers free use of design software for print book layout.

- Errors occur during conversion for print and for ebooks: a formatted file should be carefully proofread before being released onto a retail site.

Uploading to retailers:

Whether you convert your own file or pay someone else to do it for you, once it is in the appropriate format, it is a straightforward process of following instructions on the relevant site, but there are aspects it is helpful to know about:

Although Amazon is the major retail player, other distribution/retailing channels offer additional benefits, and you can sell through more than one:

- The major distribution/retailing channels for ebooks are: Amazon (Kindle Direct Publishing KDP), Kobo (Writing Life), Barnes and Noble (Nook), Apple (iBookstore) and Smashwords; and for print books: CreateSpace (Amazon) and Lightning Source.

- Each site will automatically distribute to a number of international online stores.

- Costs for uploading files vary. Some options are free; others include set-up fees and small annual retainers (especially for print).

- In setting the selling price for your book, be guided by the price of other books of similar length on your subject, and if publishing both digital and print editions, price the ebook significantly lower than the paperback. It is better to sell 10 books at US$4.99 than 2 at US$9.99. (Distributor/retailer commission charges can vary widely from around 15% to 40% of a book's retail price).

- When you select categories for your book's listing (you are generally allowed two), look at similar books to yours and think carefully about this because it is through searching these categories that browsers discover your book: that's where readers of your topic will see it.

- When you upload, install a 'Look Inside' or sampling feature, if available, so that people can read the beginning of your book and see how good it is. This is why your introduction and first chapter are critical.

- Some distributors' sites provide 'author pages' where you can post your bio and other details you want readers to know. You don't have to complete this at the time of uploading, but it's a good idea to do so at some point.

You will have to decide whether to publish your book as an ebook, or as a print-on-demand (POD) paperback, or both. Digital books offer several advantages to a self-publishing author: they are cheaper to produce; they can be uploaded and available almost immediately; they can be distributed globally almost as quickly, and once listed, they can be downloaded by a purchaser instantly. For example, Smashwords automatically distributes its author's books to Apple iBookstore's 50 international outlets: whatever corner of the world you live in, if you have access to the internet, your book can be for sale in a global market within days.

Modern readers expect digital editions of books, but many still prefer print, especially for reference and practical nonfiction works, and in some countries, digital reading is not yet well developed. It is advisable to publish both, but you can publish an ebook first to see how it sells, and a print edition later, or vice versa.

Further considerations for distributing paperback editions –

• In theory, Lightning Source distributes also to physical bookshops because it works through the international wholesaler Ingrams, but in practice, few major shops are willing to stock, or even accept orders, for print-on-demand books. (This is likely to change if more publishers use POD, and distributors start to offer bookshops the same deals for POD books as they do for other print stock).

• If you create a print edition of your book through Lightning Source or CreateSpace, it is listed by the online retailer The Book Depository (TBD) as well as Amazon's main site. Since TBD ships paperbacks to customers worldwide without any freight charge, this expands your potential market, especially if local bookstores don't stock your book. (Although TBD has been bought by Amazon, the free-freight policy continues at present).

- Print books cost more to produce than ebooks, even with POD, which is reflected in their selling price.

Nonfiction books often contain a large number of pictures. If you have written a travelogue or a book on art, for example, and you want it lavishly illustrated, you should consider the following:

- Lightning Source offers colour for illustrations, but colour is significantly more expensive in print. Balance the cost against the price readers would pay by either reducing the number of pictures, or considering black and white.

- You can include as many colour photographs as you like in an ebook – the conversion and set-up for good quality is trickier, but the additional cost is minimal.

- Up to now, e-readers, like the Kindle, are only in black and white, but tablets, e.g. Kindle Fire and iPad show books in full colour and allow readers to expand images. Amazon's free software to read Kindle books on a computer is also in colour.

- Photographs should be of high resolution – publish only your best images, (and if using someone else's, ensure you have permission to publish them).

What I have described so far is a brief overview, so that you have an idea what is involved before you decide on your options. Details change, technologies and services are continually being developed: you should study each provider and procedure further if you opt for this publishing route. For example, for print editions, some self-publishing service companies offer the option of printing book stocks (the usual minimum is 100 copies), which they warehouse and distribute to bookshops on your behalf, on a 'sale or return' basis (in the same way as mainstream publishers). This avoids the main disadvantage of print-on-demand: that a bookshop owner has to pay for a book outright with no option to return it if he cannot sell it. A warehousing and distribution service is considerably more expensive than options employing POD, but your book is more likely to be stocked by high street bookshops.

Many authors find the process much simpler and easier than might appear from the above, especially for a manuscript of simple text. But before you commit to doing it all yourself, shop around to see what various self-publishing services offer, consult other authors who have self-published, and read further into the subject. A useful source of information is the Alliance of Independent Authors (ALLi), whose web address is listed in the Appendix.

The business side of self-publishing:

Indie publishing can become an absorbing and time-consuming business. How deeply you want to be immersed in maximising sales and developing an author presence depends on your initial aims. If the existence of your published book already provides a boost to your career, or is a promotional tool to your business, you may gain as much by strategically distributing it yourself as you would from public sales.

On the other hand, if your aim is to launch and develop a career as a nonfiction author and/or freelance writer, you will want to make the most of the opportunity to establish your professional reputation. In that case, you should start thinking about your next book. The reason so many fiction authors write trilogies or series, is that it takes two or three books to build up a following and be noticed in the market. Sales of the first couple of titles may be meagre, but by the third, if the author becomes popular, readers will buy their earlier books as well.

Nonfiction books tend to be one-off, but some subjects are suitable for a series approach. A book of amusing travel experiences – e.g. 'Confessions of a Travelling Photographer' – could be published in three parts: three ebooks each approximately 30,000 words. This could also work with a history or art series, provided the first book motivated readers to want more.

A possibility for how-to topics is to write a series of short books – 15-20,000 words – each focusing on a specific aspect. For example, a series on home maintenance might include separate books on 'how to fix leaks', 'redecorating', 'storage ideas' – the scope is broad. Once you find a way of appealing to your audience, you could develop a following of loyal readers. The same applies to gardening, health and fitness, household budgeting, computer games – almost any popular activity.

If your main purpose is to earn an income, this is not a particularly realistic goal from writing, but a few have achieved it. If you are doing it all yourself, maximising profits involves checking sales figures daily; playing around with trade-offs between adjusting the price and the effects that has on different retailers' discounts; offering the book free for a period, running online competitions and a whole range of other 'all-out' marketing approaches.

You will be competing with seasoned professionals. Like any other business, self-publishing successfully requires time, expertise and resources. To reduce financial risks, you might also want to investigate sources of funding to cover part, or all, of your publishing costs through sponsorship – by organisations who share an interest in the subject of your book, for example – or through 'crowd-funding' sites such as Kickstart, Unbound and Pubslush (web addresses for these sites are in the Appendices).

To self-publish a well-turned-out nonfiction book, and make a profit, takes a lot of commitment. The choice is yours, but make sure you are well informed before you start the process.

Privately printing and distributing your book:

Print-on-demand is the easiest and quickest way to produce a printed book. Using new digital printing technology, a printer works from your electronic file, creates a lay-out and prints however many copies you require. The file is retained at your request so that further copies can be printed on demand.

Although POD is favoured by major online self-publishing services like CreateSpace, and Lightning Source, it is also available from larger commercial printers and I discuss it separately here as a method of producing your own book rather than publication on the wider market.

The electronic file containing your manuscript must be laid-out into a book before it can be printed. Book design – cover, paper, fonts, margins, page and chapter headings – is a specialised area of art and technology with its own professional standards. Designing their own book is not something amateurs should attempt without a great deal of thought, especially for a nonfiction work that might contain charts, illustrations and other graphics. Specialist software can be bought and the skills learned, but failure to reach a professional standard could scupper your writing efforts.

Some companies specialise in book printing and offer a full design service, applying your own artwork to the book cover or providing that, too, at additional cost. For private distribution, or as a heritage item for family and friends, quality of the finished product is likely to be your main concern and POD the most appropriate method of production. Additional copies can easily be printed if interest is wider than you expected.

For memoirs, local and family histories, or other topics related to your area, local bookshops and other outlets might be persuaded to stock your book, and POD would be a good option for this kind of local marketing. You would, in effect, be 'warehousing' and distributing your own book, and could offer 'sale or return' conditions to local bookshops.

The two situations where offset (lithographic) printing would be preferable is if your book contains a large number of photographs (because the quality is better), or if you want to order more than, say, 300 books at one time, for which the print run would be cheaper than POD.

Identify commercial and book printers in your region – most will have websites – and see what services they offer. Ask to see samples of their products to assess quality, and ask previous clients about their experience with the company, especially concerning accuracy, delivery times and hidden costs.

When you ask for a quotation (preferably from two or three different companies), you will be asked to specify number and size of pages, quality (weight) of paper, number of illustrations and whether in colour or black and white, type of binding and the print-run, as well as the extent of services you require (e.g. cover design). Most of these will be negotiable later if you want to upgrade the quality or reduce costs: what is important is to ensure your initial specifications are exactly the same for each company, so that you can compare their prices.

Ideally, you need to see and handle books they have produced because cheapest is rarely 'best' in book production. Your choices will depend on your aim in writing the book in the first place.

Considerations for constructing an index, designing a book cover, and writing the blurb to be included on the back, are the same as described in the previous section. Various online 'self-publishing services' also offer book design and/or printing as a paid service, but check their terms and conditions carefully to ensure you are getting only the assistance you want and are not committing yourself to anything further.

If you decide, later, to broaden the distribution of your book and to sell it more widely, you can follow the self-publishing procedures discussed earlier, and select the most appropriate marketing techniques from the next chapter – many of them are useful even for limited local distribution.

What to do now:

Whichever publishing option you wish to pursue –

→ Write your synopsis and proposal. You will edit them for specific purposes, but they are key documents with many applications in the future however your book is published.

→ Review your goals and the resources available to you. Research the publishing options to be clear on what is involved, and discuss with others, or seek advice, on the most appropriate publishing method for your work.

→ Work out a strategy to implement your chosen route, remembering to keep your options open for as long as possible.

→ Obtain professional advice before signing contracts.

WRITING YOUR NONFICTION BOOK

To buy a full publishing package –

→ Identify the companies who offer this service and study their terms and conditions carefully; check what others say about their experience before committing yourself.

→ Continue to build your author platform, and study the next chapter on marketing to begin planning your promotion strategy.

To pursue traditional publishing –

→ Research publishers and/or agents and draw up your list of 'targets'.

→ It will help you to stay organised if you construct a table listing the people/companies you intend to approach, with columns to record when queries or submissions are sent and replies received.

→ Adjust your letters and other submission contents to target each agent/publisher specifically.

→ While you wait for responses, continue to develop your author platform and start reading Chapter 9 on setting up the basic tools for marketing.

To self-publish your book –

→ Make a plan: decide whether you want a print or digital publication, or both; list the main tasks involved – formatting, cover, and so on – and identify for which stages you will need professional input.

→ Do some internet searches on blogs and websites of self-publishing/author services, self-publishing forums, and indie authors, to gain insights into the whole process, and the support that may be available to you. You could make significant contacts in the process.

→ Research providers for the assistance you require, obtaining quotes and references, and compile a contact list of those you decide to employ.

→ Draw up a budget of likely total costs (allow for marketing and promotion), and work out your financing.

→ Draft a programme: you are running a project that involves everything from service providers to online retailers, so work out a timetable for each stage, recording when work is commissioned and returned, and the progress on tasks you decide to implement yourself.

→ Read quickly through the next chapter on marketing before you begin implementing your project: if you know what is involved, it enables you to carry out some forward planning and budgeting, and perhaps pick up opportunities you discover in your early searches.

9.

Market Your Book

Understand what marketing is:

Marketing is not synonymous with selling: sales are the desired outcome of a whole range of longer-term marketing activities and considerations, most of which do not directly involve selling. The other mantra from the professionals is: we don't sell products we sell 'benefits' – what the purchaser gains from buying.

Look at advertisements for almost anything and you'll notice they focus first on the customers' wants and how the product satisfies them, not on describing the product – that comes second but with the same angle towards advantages for the purchaser. This is why big companies spend millions on gathering customers' household profiles; it enables them to assess what appeals to different categories of people.

Many authors, because they are creative, artistic people, fear what they think of as the commercial circus of marketing. But it is not an alien world: it begins with you, your book, and the readers for whom you wrote it – all familiar to you. What marketing achieves is to make them familiar to others too, so that they are aware of your book and the benefits they gain from reading it.

We now come full circle to the work you did in Chapter 1 – identifying your purpose, the readers you are 'talking' to, and the genre of your work – because, along with your decision as to which publishing route to follow, these are the foundation of a marketing strategy for your book. The main processes in marketing a book involve:

- A quality product – a well-written manuscript/book

- The creator of the product – you, the author, your credibility and accessibility

- Presentation of both product and creator – (from book cover to your blog design)

- Customers you wish to attract – agents, publishers, bookstores, readers, media

- Places where the work will be noticed – 'discoverability' online and elsewhere

- Promotion to increase awareness – both the content and media targeted

- The price and mechanism for sales – balancing competitiveness with profitability

- Partnerships with those implementing the various marketing processes

How directly you are involved in each of these aspects depends on whether you are offering a manuscript to agents and publishers, or seeking customers for a published book, but the key to them all is building relationships and in this you will definitely need to play an active role.

All publishers these days expect authors to participate in a marketing strategy; some only consider authors who have already developed a public presence – an author platform. If you are self-publishing, you will be carrying out your own marketing, which may include hiring professional assistance. In a market where approximately 150,000 new print books were published in 2011 in the UK alone, identifying and selectively applying your advantages in the most effective manner is essential, and for that you need to plan.

A huge amount is written about book marketing, especially doing so online because for digital books, that is where most readers do their browsing and seek information. It is easy to become obsessed with pushing your book and trying to appear on every social network and relevant blog, dissipating your efforts in a vast web where everyone else is doing the same. This is like shouting alone in a forest, when, in fact, you should be finding allies to cut a path with you between the trees.

A marketing strategy is a long-term process of building quality relationships with identified groups of people who share your interest: those who publish and/or read your genre. It is about creating awareness and establishing a reputation because without these, people don't know you, or your book, exist, let alone be willing to invest their time and effort. And you don't have to be an all-singing, all-dancing extrovert – project the real person you are, the author who wrote a unique book.

If you have followed each step with me so far, you have achieved by now a thoroughly prepared manuscript, a decision as to how you will pursue its publication and the beginnings of an author platform as described in Chapter 7; you are clear on your purpose, readers and genre, and you have already drafted a proposal and synopsis, brief summaries of each chapter and a 1,000-word article. You have something special to offer: your own marketing strategy is built with all of these, whether you do it alone or with a publisher, so this is our starting point.

There is no simple 'to-do' list which suits every situation. Your specific actions and where you apply them depends on your own circumstances, the nature of your book and your means of publication, so the remainder of this chapter describes options and how to implement them. From these tools you construct your marketing plan, but be realistic: results take time and some approaches may work better for you than others. Above all, view this stage positively – you can be as creative in marketing as you can in writing.

In essence, when we market our work, we apply our own personality and expertise to nurture our book's unique character, to animate its attributes and enable it to perform in public. What exactly that performance consists of depends on the book's nature, and how effective the performance is depends on the suitability of the audience. Bear these three key aspects in mind as you assess marketing possibilities: the potential in yourself, your book and your audience. If you have already found an agent or a publisher, these three aspects are what you contribute to the overall marketing effort.

You need two important resources ready before you start marketing:

- Author bios – not merely one, a selection of varying lengths: 12 words; 50 words; 100 words and 250 words. You will be asked for any one of them by different media for various purposes. Take time to construct each one to convey the most important information. When you are asked for a bio, edit it again to target that publication's readers.

- Book blurbs – you need a selection of these, too, from a collection of 6-word headlines or tag-lines, to100-word and 250-word synopses. They can all be used on websites, in tweets, or by journalists to save them time and effort, and if they use your blurb as copy, it ensures the book is described in the way you would prefer.

To convey information, enticement, emotional appeal and benefits all at once with so few words is not easy: it is better to write them in advance, editing when required, than to be pressured by a sudden request and throw something together in a hurry.

Participating in social media:

The range of social media sites is huge and growing. Given that the most effective means of engaging social media for building a reputation is by interacting with other users, trying to belong to all of them will either spread your efforts too thinly, or run you to a state of exhaustion.

If you laid the foundations for a social media presence by starting a Twitter account as recommended in Chapter 7, you need only expand your following and increase your interactions in preparation for linking followers to your blog once it is set up. If you are already on Facebook, you can socialise on that, too, especially if you have photographs to post on your 'wall'. (But don't post more than a couple of the photographs you will include in your book: only people who buy the book should have access to those. It is part of the value of what they purchase). Whatever network you are already involved in, I recommend participating on Twitter in conjunction with a blog.

I discuss setting up a blog below, but before leaving Twitter, there is one particularly helpful technique you can use there: pitching.

Pitching:

In common usage, a 'pitch' is the spot where a street seller or market trader sets up a stall and calls out their wares to attract passing trade. In publishing, authors also call out their wares – their proposals, manuscripts or books – but not in a static location. The difference is that each pitch, each call, is targeted precisely to the publisher, agent or group of readers they wish to attract. And it can be made verbally, via email or letter, through social media or even on a brief video on YouTube, depending on the target for the pitch.

When you write a covering letter to a publisher, or a query letter to an agent, you are pitching your manuscript, but the technique can be used in many other ways for promoting your published book.

With the scramble for attention in a highly competitive publishing world, the essence of a good pitch is brevity. Someone may give you only ten seconds of their attention in which to make an impact. In your searches of writing sites, you may have come across the American term 'elevator pitch'. The idea is to construct a pitch that can be made in the brief time shared with someone going up in a lift. Not the likeliest place to make such an approach, but it's a good way of demonstrating the process.

Imagine that a stranger and you step into a lift together; she's standing by the button panel asking which floor you want. You want the cafeteria, she does, too.

Stranger: "Lunch break?"

You: "No, meeting an agent to talk about my book."

Stranger: "Yeah? What's your book about?"

You: "It's a cookery book. It has sixty recipes for menus that [*the stranger taps on her smartphone and starts checking her messages...*] enable you to stay healthy and live a long life because they help you to lose..." [*voice fades*].

All cookery books contain recipes. You spent half your listener's attention span telling her nothing and she tuned out.

Take two:

Stranger: "Yeah? What's your book about?"

You: "Food that helps you lose weight. [*The stranger listens.*] Sixty easy, delicious meals that keep you healthy."

Stranger: "Wow! Where can I find it?"

Almost everyone loves food, wants to lose weight by eating rather than dieting, and is short of time. She'll probably buy your book and tell her friends she met the author.

People can ask what your book is about at any time: be ready with your ten-second pitch. And in case you hadn't noticed, the successful response above takes up eighty-one characters, including spaces. If you tweeted it, there would be fifty-nine characters remaining for a recipient's @name and a hashtag – #food. This is 'pitch thinking' and to do it you need to retain the essential benefits of your book at the top of your mind.

I don't suggest you pitch other Tweeters at random – that rightly annoys people – but if you share progress on your book, or a release date, for example, someone may ask what your book is about. Once you relate to people in a general way, opportunities to pitch in a friendly, un-pushy manner emerge naturally.

Review the brief chapter summaries, the synopsis and the blurb you wrote earlier. Pick out significant phrases and edit them to create a series of different pitches that would fit into a tweet, or take ten seconds of someone's time at a social or professional gathering. If you arouse your listener's curiosity, you'll have the chance to tell them more about it, like where they can buy it. Brief, succinct answers maintain interest. If you begin the long story, they'll probably stop listening and forget you even wrote a book.

This kind of pitch is like a 'tag-line' (or 'logline') – the brief phrase you see on film billboards designed to attract a viewer's attention with some special feature of the film – and can be displayed in the same way as a headline or catch-phrase on your website or blog.

Promoting through blogging:

Both websites and blogs occupy a named location on the Internet, a display space to showcase who you are and what you do, but they are not the same thing. A website is static: it may have several pages, each containing different types of information, and one of them may be a 'contact' page where a viewer can email the site owner, but they are essentially hoardings which are updated irregularly.

A blog is designed to be active and interactive: 'posts' – brief articles, updates, images and features – are added frequently, sometimes daily, more commonly, weekly, and viewers are encouraged to leave comments on each post with the aim of developing on-going discussions, which attract new followers to the blog. Your blog is a responsive marketing tool; a place for communicating with your book's potential readers. It is like a combined office, reception and showroom for visitors which could include anyone from a film director and publisher's editor, to readers from your local library, or indeed, your computer-savvy grandmother.

However, a website can contain a 'blog' as one of its pages and, in this way, provide the same regular updates, posts, and visitor participation.

To create a blog, you work with one of the many 'platforms' or 'hosting services'. To keep it simple, I discuss below only the two largest and most popular platforms.

The basics of setting up a blog:

The two main providers of blogging platforms are WordPress (wordpress.com) and Blogger (blogspot.com, which is owned and controlled by Google). They are both free, guide you through the set-up process with clear instructions, offer a choice of design themes, and provide similar possibilities, but WordPress has more options for customising the appearance and adding gadgets, and many writers choose it for a more professional look. But few goods are truly 'free', and both platforms are operated by massive organisations, each with their own terms and conditions with which users must comply, so check these out before you make your choice.

You might prefer an independent option through WordPress.org – a different set-up to WordPress.com – which you can either host yourself, or have hosted by a professional webmaster who will oversee the security of your site and its visibility to search engines. The potential for customisation with WordPress.org is almost limitless, and it has the capacity to create a sophisticated website which includes a blog, so you can have the best of both worlds, with scope for future development. Creating and maintaining an independent site requires technical skills that are beyond the majority of users, so most people employ a professional host organisation.

Hosting for an independent site is a paid service, and the cost will increase gradually the more content you post (especially if you display a lot of images) and the more visitors you attract, but you may decide it is worth the set-up and annual retaining fee to exercise full control of the site and have someone to sort out technical problems. Web-hosting services are often web/blog designers as well, and able to set up your blog to your specifications. Costs vary, so obtain quotes, and ask others for recommendations.

Whichever platform you choose, begin by browsing other authors' blogs and note features you find useful and attractive. If you hire a professional to set up your blog, brief them fully on the impression you want your site to give to viewers and show them links to blogs you like. Begin by asking yourself the same questions about purpose and readers that you asked when planning the book, because a blog also represents a body of original work – published on the Internet – and readers will only return a second time if they find it a pleasant experience of value to them. Above all, your blog needs to be easy to navigate i.e. locate different posts and features, and quick to read.

The first considerations in designing your site are:

- Acquiring a domain name: if you choose wordpress.org, you will first buy your own domain name, your unique spot on the web with a distinctive URL. It increases your visibility online if you include in the domain name, the personal name and activity you wish to be known for, e.g. 'josmithtravelwriter.com'. With wordpress.com and blogspot.com you are on their domains: the URL of your blog will include 'wordpress.com', or 'blogspot.com' (the suffix varies according to which country you register for), but both allow you to pay an annual fee to use your own domain name instead.

- Blog name and header image: both should relate to your topic of interest and the main fact about you that you wish to project, e.g. author, subject specialism, business interest. Your blog is easier to recognise and find if your own name (or the name you write under) and your interests are incorporated in the name and header of your blog, so it is a good idea to use part of your domain name for your blog's title. (Ideally, your Twitter profile, domain name and blog title will all have some recognisable feature in common).

- Overall theme and appearance: busy and colourful? Calm and thoughtful? Containing images symbolising what you do? The theme you choose creates the first impression for a visitor; it needs to be enticing and memorable. Keep it simple – conveying one strong, clear message – and select text that is easy to read.

- Pages: the number of pages you can create depends on which platform you use, but the basic pages you need are: HOME/BLOG (usually where people 'land' after clicking your URL and a good place for your tag-line); ABOUT for your bio and/or mission statement for the site, and CONTACT to enable readers to email you (it's a good idea to set up a dedicated email address for this).

- Special features: if your platform host offers the capacity, you might also create a page specifically about your book; a gallery of pictures, or some other special feature – I made a page for the tree house which features in my web address and header image, and also on my Twitter Profile.

My own blog is part of my website which is professionally hosted, and operates from WordPress.org. I post on a separate BLOG page, but also insert occasional brief news updates (upcoming books, new releases), on my HOME page (the landing page) along with a brief 'welcome' message saying how often and what type of material I post. However your blog is arranged, the first permanent item on the landing page should be a 'welcome', and your tag-line, or a phrase that tells browsers immediately what the site is about. Mine reads: *'Welcome to the Treehouse: writing…travel…books…photographs'*.

For each of your pages, you can select from a range of widgets, plug-ins and other buttons and links that encourage your readers to participate in some way, or connect with you on other online networks. The most important of these are:

- Follow: link-buttons that connect readers to follow you on Twitter, Facebook or wherever else you interact.

- Share: with as many options as possible to enable readers to disseminate a post to others in their networks: an effective way to increase 'traffic' – the number of visitors to your site. Locate share buttons on each blog post as well as each page.

- Subscribe: an opt-in provision for readers to subscribe to your blog, automatically receiving notice of new postings via email or other automatic 'feed' system.

- Comment: the process for leaving comments needs to be easy, but a screening device that enables you to approve and moderate comments before they become public, is advisable to control spam.

- Recent posts/popular posts: listed down a side panel, this encourages viewers to read earlier posts.

- Categories: lists your posts under topics you choose, making it easier for readers to find topics of interest to them

What to blog about:

To be effective in promoting your work, a blog needs to be professional-looking, active with regular new material, and discoverable among millions of other blogs on the Internet.

Interesting, original content is essential, and regularity builds up a following whether you post weekly (optimal for many bloggers and readers) or every two or three weeks. Short posts are more effective: 300-500 words can entertain and inform; 1,000 words can give depth to a more complex subject; few browsers will read more than that. In fact, most skim-read at speed, so write in short paragraphs placing the most important bits at the beginning of the piece, and in the first line of each subsequent paragraph. And start with a 'hook' to grab people's attention. Blogging is an excellent way to develop writing skills.

If you've designed your blog with a theme that supports your book and major interest, and posted a tag-line on the landing page, these condition readers' expectations of what to find on the site, so your posts will focus generally around that theme, but they can still be varied in content and angle. Here are some suggestions of what to blog about:

- You, the author: posts on why, how, where, when you wrote the book and events you attend – signings, launches, interviews, etc. quote brief extracts but don't blog too much of your book or more than one or two of its illustrations.

- You, the person: whatever you feel comfortable in sharing about your work and life – readers like learning about the authors they read. (Be aware of security: avoid details that identify exactly where you live and especially when you might be away).

- Place: for travel, history, memoir and biography, opportunities for writing about related places are many, but everything happens somewhere, and almost any topic has a location reference that can be made intriguing and interesting.

- Time: the same applies to times past in relation to your topic, e.g.

what your travel destination was like in the past, how crafts were produced, or illnesses treated a hundred years ago, especially if you have access to old photographs. Whatever your topic, an old postcard of a local landmark could generate an evocative brief article.

- People: stories about historical figures; people met on your travels – a post about market traders, for example; notable influences connected to your special subject. If you write on local history, persuade a few local 'characters' to let you interview them and edit the transcripts as 'blog interviews', or as profile pieces.

- Information: updates or details about your area of expertise – new developments, techniques, events.

- Photo-essays: a collection of pictures around a theme that requires few words but can create a mood consistent with the theme of your book.

- Reviews: reviews of other people's books that reflect your principle interests. Rather than feel awkward about reviewing a title that competes with yours, select authors that approach the subject from an entirely different perspective. Don't restrict yourself to nonfiction: a historian could review a historical novel or a scientist comment on science fiction, attracting a new audience to their site.

- Interviews: other authors may be willing to participate in blog interviews (usually worked out via email): a good way to forge online relationships.

- Humour: use humour where appropriate – funny anecdotes, disastrous DIY projects, pets' antics – people love to find something to laugh at and lift their day. If your book is about dogs or cats – always a popular topic – your own pet's foibles provide an endless supply of ideas. The same applies to children and parenting.

- Topical issues: mark national and international celebrations, commemorations and special events, or comment on current news items, by offering your own unique angle.

The title of a blog post should be short and descriptive, and the first line something that grabs our attention because these are the headlines (as in a newspaper). They are picked up by search engines to display when people search specific topics with key words. Google loves numbers, lists and bullet points: '10 ways to…', '5 Things you…', and 'How to…' which you should take full advantage of if writing about practical skills. But even for history, a post might be about '5 Reasons to Love History', or for travel, '10 Packing Tips for Trips'. But vary the posts: you're a writer – an author – demonstrate your style and skill.

Images increase the attractiveness of posts. Include at least one relevant picture placed alongside the heading, either your own photograph or one downloaded from a free-photo site. Always attribute the original photographer and be careful not to post a picture that is copyright or you could be in trouble for infringement.

And always, always, edit and proofread your posts to eliminate spelling or grammatical errors: your blog is a public window on your work; it needs to show you at your best. The same approach to presentation (and to libel, liability, plagiarism and copyright) applies to a blog as to any other medium of publication.

If you need a push-start, retrieve that 1,000-word article you wrote at the beginning and edit it into one or more blog posts, or review your original timeline, pick out items you didn't include in your book, or only briefly, and develop those into short posts.

Other ways to make the most of your blog and/or website for marketing (depending what is possible from your particular site):

- Include a permanent display of your book cover and a brief description, or a ten-second pitch

- Install 'Buy' buttons that link to your book at online retail sites: especially effective for self-published authors. Place it beneath a picture of the book cover, or embed it in the image.

- Sell directly: with a secure payment arrangement such as PayPal, privately published books can be sold directly online independently of retailers.

- Quote your blog/website address with other contact details as part of your signature when emailing, and add it to your business card and letter head.

The popularity of a blog builds up gradually. Responding promptly to comments people leave on your site, and visiting and commenting on other people's blogs, helps to build a network of mutually interested readers. As more readers participate, it becomes a bit like an online party each time you post a new piece; if you enjoy the experience, it shows in your writing. Blogging is a long-term strategy: to maintain your motivation, it must bring you pleasure and satisfaction. If you find the whole process unmitigated hell, even after persevering for a few months, it is best to stop and focus on other marketing ideas. We all possess different strengths.

Nearly everywhere you click on the Internet someone is offering advice about blogging. Don't be overawed by urgings to write with SEO (Search Engine Optimisation) in mind; to check your visitor statistics daily, and to worry about your Google ranking (i.e. whether your blog appears on page one or page four of a search). This advice is aimed at online businesses and those seeking to earn from their blogs as channels for advertising: their main objective is to generate income.

Such approaches might be of interest to you if your book's purpose is to boost your business or career, or you are engaged in 'all-out' marketing for a self-published book, but for most authors, their goal is to showcase their work and build a community of readers who share their interests and may, at some point, buy their books and recommend them to their friends – long-term reputation building rather than short-term selling.

However you operate your blog, the time and effort is wasted if no one is aware of its existence. Use Twitter to promote it by announcing when new posts are added; put a link to that post in your tweet and attach a relevant hashtag. You can repeat the process a couple of times a day for a few days by changing the wording of the announcement – refer to your collection of tag-lines to write catchy, interesting tweets with your link.

Writing guest posts –

Once your blog-writing skills are developed, consider offering articles to other sites as a 'guest post' to extend your exposure and promotion potential. For the recipient, these are free copy and opportunities are plentiful, especially on special-interest sites focusing, for example, on the environment, health, travel destinations, or business. The host usually lets guests include a brief bio and their blog address, and even a link to a book. They look for well-written posts which contain value for their readers, but you should check out their sites carefully. If few people visit them, you gain little for your effort.

Look also at their HOME and ABOUT pages and what other articles they display to make sure it is a site with which you are happy to be publicly associated.

Online newspapers –

Before we leave the marketing potential of social media and the Web, I want to share another idea: create your own daily online newspaper. This is much easier than you might think, because a company called paper.li offers a service that makes the compilation almost automatic – and it's free. I know grandmothers who edit their daily online paper and tweet the link to their followers before making porridge in the morning.

You can learn more about it by visiting the paper.li site http://paper.li/ and clicking on the 'see how it works' link. Paper.li screens 250 million social media posts per day from all the main networks, accessing 25 million articles, videos and images. Daily online papers provide links to a selection of posts that relate to specific subjects chosen by the editor.

When you set up a paper-li account, you choose which networks to draw from as a source, and what topics interest you. These are automatically compiled, downloaded and laid out into a standard format, but you can edit what appears, and write a brief editorial if you wish. And you can, of course, include a link to your own blog posts, complete with photograph, in the prime position: the top left-hand corner.

For the paper's title you can use your own name – 'The John Smith Daily', or a phrase more descriptive of content, for a cane weaver, perhaps, 'The Basket Case Daily'. You could also incorporate part of your book's title, but the paper's title should be short to leave room for a good tag-line when you tweet out the link. And it is acceptable to tweet the link directly @ anyone whose post or photo is in the paper: this is free publicity for them and they are likely to share it with their followers on their own networks, which is good promotion for you.

Writing press releases:

As with all important communication, when sending a press release we should first understand the point of view of the recipient and draft it accordingly. To busy newspaper and magazine editors, press releases are an easy source of copy and the nearer they are to 'print ready' when received, the more likely they are to be used. But 'stories' must be of interest to their particular readers.

Publishers' press officers are aware of this and of the styles of individual publications; if you work through a publisher, they will write the initial press release, drawing upon information you provided. If you self-publish, you are your own publicist. But press releases are not only for announcing a new book; learn to write them and you can issue them to attract media coverage of any promotional event you organise later.

For press releases, adjust your writing style to that of journalism: factual, clear and concise, with a headline to grab attention, short paragraphs and all key information in the first half of the text. Media editors don't have time to fiddle about with the kind of editing you applied to the manuscript: if a piece is too long for the space available, they simply cut the bottom paragraph, or two. If you wrote something essential there, it's gone.

Other important style features are to write in the third person and to quote direct speech a couple of times to give the piece immediacy, authenticity and emotional appeal: "What happened to me has preyed on my mind for fifteen years," said author, Sandy Plonk. "I just had to write it down."

Keep your press release to one page and remember that both newspapers and magazines depend for their income on advertising: they will not accept a 'story' that is a thinly disguised advertisement for your book trying to slip in for free. But there is a subtle difference in perspective between newspapers and magazines when it comes to content, so I'll discuss them separately.

Most local and regional newspapers are published daily, or twice weekly, a few weekly; they are interested in *news* – something significant and novel that, preferably, no one else knows about yet. The publication of your book is, naturally, big news to *you*, but you need to find an angle that makes it newsworthy to others. Can you link your book to a current piece of news or local event? Is there something about the book or about your achievements that is 'the first time' or 'the only' (other than it being your first book)? Does it contain a special 'human story' that relates to the locality?

These same considerations apply equally to local radio and television stations, which also accept press releases and should be included in your promotion plan.

Magazines, however, work on a longer time-frame as most are published monthly or quarterly, and often less focused on a particular locality. Because magazine editors plan their features months in advance, immediate newsworthiness may be less important than the interest and significance of the subject. Whatever you write about, there is bound to be a magazine covering that topic (browse the racks in your local newsagent). Readers of specialist magazines are interested in new techniques or recent findings relevant to their subject niche and probably consider them more newsworthy than would the general readers of a newspaper.

Magazines are also more likely to use the information in your press release for writing their own feature or possibly for a review. In your press release, increase the appeal of your book by linking it, if you can, to a relevant commemorative event; the anniversary of a well-known figure; an 'International Day of…', or an annual celebration or cultural event. Most magazines publish special features to mark such occasions according to their particular focus, but submit your press release six months before the event.

In addition to the subtle difference between newspapers and magazines in what constitutes 'news', the content of your press release should target the specific interests of each publication, bearing in the mind their regular readership. For all of them, though, there is a set pattern for presentation and core information that should be included in a press release.

Presenting a press release:

- Write in Times New Roman 12 point font, lines double spaced on a single sheet of A4 (for hard copy, if you can't fit in a vital piece of information, it is better to use 1.5 spacing than to spread over two pages; if emailing, a couple of extra lines don't matter).

- Centred at the top and in bold capitals write: **PRESS RELEASE**

- Below that aligned left: **For immediate release: (date)** if you want it published as soon as possible, or **Embargoed until: (time/date)** if you want them to wait, for example, for the release date of your book. But 'immediate release' is better: they might forget in the meantime.

- Centred and in bold, write your headline: a six-word pitch that immediately grabs attention with what the release is about and why it is news: 'Our secrets revealed by local historian', 'Teenager scoops mega book deal'. Study newspapers, see how they do it.

- Compose the main text, comprising three or four short paragraphs: write key information in the first paragraph, followed by essential expansion and a couple of brief quotes (e.g. from you and another relevant source), with other desirable but less critical information in the final paragraph. All should be written in the third person.

- Be as concise as possible; cut and redraft repeatedly to fit the most interesting and newsworthy aspects of the story onto the page.

- At the end of the text, aligned left, write: Ends

- Optional line, aligned left beneath the text and in bold: **Note to Editors**: indicate briefly what else is available, e.g. photographs, review copy of the book, author interview, date of author event (launch, reading, demonstration).

- Aligned left and in bold: **Contact**: provide your full name (or your author name if different) email address and phone number where you can be reached 24 hours a day – newspapers and newsrooms work night shifts.

Call the paper or radio station to check whether they prefer press releases in hard copy or email (more usual). For hard copy, enclose prints of your book cover and 'portrait style' photo of yourself, clearly labelled on the back with your name and contact details (write on adhesive labels: pressure on the back of photographs causes damage). If emailing, write 'PR: + your headline' in the subject line and paste your press release into the body of the email, not as an attachment. And I advise against attaching jpeg images of your cover and yourself: many publications do not accept unsolicited attachments of any kind and the email may bounce back or be deleted unread. They need higher resolution pictures anyway if they decide to run the story: a good reason for you to be easily contactable.

Follow up a couple of days later by calling the news-desk to check if they received your press release. If possible, find out which reporter or journalist is dealing with it and whether you can speak to them. If you do, ask if your piece will be used and whether he/she needs any further information. Keep your conversation short and avoid ringing media people first thing in the morning (they've probably been up half the night), or in the afternoon when they are frantically chasing deadlines.

You can send press releases to several different papers and radio stations at one time. And if a reporter calls you for an interview – as happened to me while I was writing this chapter – ask what time suits them, and, if at all possible, drop everything and be there when they want you. Journalists work to deadlines; if your story misses this one, someone else's may have taken over the news by the next edition and yours could be dropped. Remember to take your book, and leave a flyer, bio, synopsis and business card with the journalist so she can check the facts if she can't read her notes. They are likely to photograph you, so take a comb as well.

Requesting book reviews:

If you are working with a publisher, at least six months before publication, they will ask you to complete an Author's Publicity Form to list, among other things, your professional and personal contacts and any organisations or individuals who might promote or take an interest in your book. The publisher refers to this when drawing up a marketing plan, and in particular, to identify potential reviewers. Mainstream media usually require review copies several months ahead of the publication date ('review copies' are often 'proofs' i.e. produced before the final printing of a book).

But once the book is released, you can ask your publisher for additional copies to send out personally to people who are likely to appreciate it and pass on their enjoyment to others by word-of-mouth. Personal recommendation is one of the most important marketing tools.

Asking contacts to read your work and post a review on GoodReads, and on Amazon or other online retailers' sites can also be effective. Be aware though, that a rush of 5-star reviews from mums and best friends will be recognised for what they are and may do more harm than good.

If you bought a publishing package, or you are independently self-publishing, most potential reviewers will be online book bloggers, because mainstream media rarely review self-published books or anybody's ebooks. Look at your social media contacts and search for sites that review your topic, or might at least mention your book's availability if it is relevant to the site's mission. If your ebook is on Apple's iBookstores, they allow you to send up to 50 free digital review copies within a specified period after its release.

Be patient: book bloggers are inundated with review requests and may take months to read your book – some will not review it at all. When you ask for a review, write the same sort of pitch as in a blurb or cover letter and make it short, but remember it is a request and the recipient is not bound to respond. Check on the submission requirements for review sites: most prefer to be asked first, so don't send the book unless they agree to you doing so. Your community of contacts on Twitter should include book bloggers and others who share your interest: a request for review is more likely to be accepted by someone you already interact with on social media.

If you published a print edition, you might obtain quicker results by contacting local and regional papers and magazines, especially if your book contains local interest. Check whether they carry book reviews; if they do, write a letter similar to the contents of your press release, attach a synopsis and offer the editor a review copy. If they don't review it, they might interview you instead.

Whichever publishing route you are following, scan your list of professional and personal contacts: do any of them run websites, circulate a newsletter, or hold regular public meetings or events? Ask if they are willing to review, or at least announce, your book. Offer to write a short informative piece they can use in some way; to talk at a meeting, or attend an event. If you make it easy for people, they are more likely to cooperate in your request.

Other book promotion ideas:

- Submit short articles (up to 1,000 words) to print and online media relevant to your subject. Make them informative and entertaining, leave the promotion to your brief author bio – even as little as: 'Donald McDonald is the author of *Golden Age Golfers*, and lives in St Andrews' is valuable exposure if the paper's circulation is around 30,000 (as it is for the Scotsman and many regional papers in other countries).

- Suggest talks, interviews, demonstrations or filming opportunities to local radio and television stations. Find out the names of producers or journalists with an interest in your topic and pitch directly to them by name. Use the same approach as in your press release, focused on the demonstration or filming opportunity you have in mind.

- Arrange book signings and readings in bookshops – it promotes them as well as you – but you could make the event more exciting by holding it in a restaurant, bar, museum or art gallery cafeteria, public park or gardens, or any relevant venue. For ideas, think about potential readers and where they hang out.

- Identify local businesses that might display or sell your book: a garden centre, for example, for a book on growing food; a museum, hotel, tourist office or cultural centre for local histories or guides.

- Offer to talk, demonstrate, or provide one-day workshops on your subject to schools, colleges, interest groups, clubs, and libraries – and take copies of your book with you.

- Construct a brief video around your book and upload it onto YouTube, promoting it through social media. Short film has most impact: e.g. 40 seconds of intriguing and interesting images with appropriate background sound that delivers a tag-line or other message. A series of still photographs can be made into a video.

- Run competitions on your blog with copies of your book as prizes, or encourage people to subscribe to your blog by offering a draw for a free copy if they sign-up by a certain date. Promote the opportunity on your social media channels; whether people subscribe or not, it's another way to draw attention to your book.

- Look out for local events – fairs, markets, open days – where you might put up or share a stall, or give a reading. Another opportunity for a competition: 'Guess the number of words in this book.'

- Donate a copy of your book for local fund-raising raffles and draws – a way to stimulate word-of-mouth attention and feel good at the same time.

- Give copies to local libraries and ask them to display it on the 'New Acquisitions' shelf.

- Collaborate with other authors, practitioners or professionals to hold joint events, making the opportunity larger and more attractive to encourage people to attend.

- Set up a virtual launch party on your blog: especially important for self-published authors and those published only as ebooks. Advertise it in advance on Twitter and other social media networks. Include competitions and prizes, encourage comments and be on-site to respond immediately and generate a 'being there' atmosphere.

- Order and distribute business cards, bookmarks or postcards bearing images and brief quotes from your book, your contact details and blog address, and where the book is available. Libraries and bookshops are usually keen to receive free bookmarks to hand out.

- Make coloured Xerox copies of your book cover (opened out to show front and back), and treat them as flyers to display or hand out as opportunities arise – another reason why the blurb and author bio on the back should be concise and enticing.

If you are lucky, your publisher arranges book launches, sometimes more than one in different locations; a lot of copies may be sold at a launch party, resulting in personal recommendations. Launches may also attract media coverage; your publisher will certainly invite them. And, of course, you should tweet and blog about it beforehand. Extend the benefits of a launch by posting photographs and descriptions of the event afterwards.

It is well worth the effort for self-published authors to arrange their own launches. If bookshops do not stock your book (and will not, therefore, host a launch), find an alternative interesting venue that would attract readers, and order ample copies of your book available for sale.

Even though most bookshops do not stock self-published or print-on-demand books, it is worth approaching the managers of local stores because they are likely to make an exception for a local author, especially if you have attracted some media coverage, or can arrange a 'photo opportunity' in their shop.

If you are published only in digital form, suggestions above that depend on seeing or handling a physical product are not open to you, so you must be creative in adapting ideas to suit your situation. At readings, events and venues, the focus will be on your presence and what you offer directly to your audience at the time. If a promotional video is available, you could transfer it onto DVDs as a 'physical product' for strategic distribution or display; once a video has been made, it is cheap to copy.

During your personal appearances, make sure you tell people about your blog or website because, for digital books, your prime market-place where ebook readers browse, is online. Your social media and internet activities are vital. And you can expand your readership by giving helpful information: make sure people know that they don't need a special device like a Kindle or iPad to read ebooks; give them the link to Amazon's free download software – Kindle for PC – and make it easier for them to discover they can read ebooks, including yours, from their computer screen.

To make it easy for *you*, here are the web addresses: for the UK – http://amzn.to/rf41QN and for the USA and rest of the world – http://amzn.to/nuQtcH

Constructing your marketing plan:

Effective marketing applies a range of ideas – a multi-pronged approach – to attract readers in different ways and to repeat the 'message' in a variety of forms. The general pattern is that an author's reputation begins to develop well before a book is finished, and forms the platform for the focused surge of activity immediately before and during the release of their book. After this, the pace of events settles down to a 'maintenance' level of on-going promotion that combines both short-term and long-term marketing methods.

If you are carrying out much of the marketing yourself, or working without a publisher, you need to be selective about where you invest your time and energy: establish a basis for prioritising.

Study the promotion ideas above, adding others that occur to you, and draw up a list of all the possibilities that are feasible for you, bearing in mind your own strengths, the nature of your book, your readers, and the identity and whereabouts of your contacts. Divide the list into 'launch' and 'on-going'. Once you set your ideas in motion, arrangements can become quite complicated, so a good way to handle the administration of your marketing is to make a chart.

For your 'launch' chart, construct three columns: contacts, materials, and venue. Each item or event on your list will involve others, e.g. an editor you submit a press release to or a bookshop you ask to host a reading; enter their role and contact details in the 'contact' column. Materials might be copies of your book, or equipment for a demonstration; if they are required, note what you need and how/where to obtain them. Add in the 'venue' column where each event will take place and what booking arrangements are necessary (if the venue is your blog that will be easy).

Do the same for your chart of 'on-going' promotion activities. If you don't yet know the contact or the venue, write TBF (to be found) to indicate future action you must take.

Prioritise the items on both charts: your criteria might be that they require action first; they are the easiest to implement, or some other factor important to you. From this, draw up a timeline of actions you need to take, with some means of tracking when you did so and the progress on responses.

If you have written an educational or text book for a ready market that your publisher mainly deals with, your work-load for publicity and marketing will be enviably less, but many of the above activities will broaden the range of potential readers and boost your own professional reputation.

The amount of time, effort and funds you invest in promoting and marketing your book depends on your initial purpose in writing it. Whatever they are, and however you approach this stage, it is important to maintain balance and a sense of perspective. Inevitably, 99% of us will not be turned into celebrities, nor see our books staged as best sellers. We can choose either to blight our lives by chaffing against the unattainable, or we can work our corner with energy and sincerity and still make a difference in people's lives through what we write – often a much longer-term difference.

What to do now:

→ Take time to consider the options and possibilities; find what others are doing; listen to ideas, and decide what will work for you.

→ Draw up a realistic marketing plan and a timeline of actions required to implement it. Construct the 'launch' and 'on-going' charts to guide the process.

→ Identify contacts and service providers who can assist or collaborate in your efforts.

→ Work through your plan, remaining open to new ideas or opportunities that arise once you start doing so, as they surely will.

→ Celebrate every small success, learn from each setback, and stay your course.

To have written a book, especially a well-written book, is a notable achievement in its own right. We gain satisfaction not only from that, but from the knowledge that we leave a heritage for others. The journey requires both a dream and a commitment. And because I suggested in the Introduction that you should read straight through this book to view the landscape before taking the first steps on that journey, this point is your beginning. I share with you my own lantern:

"The moment one definitely commits oneself then Providence moves too. All sorts of things occur to help one that would never otherwise occur. Whatever you can do, or dream you can do, begin it. Boldness has genius, power and magic in it."

(By tradition, attributed to Johann Wolfgang von Goethe).

Acknowledgements

Book ideas have a habit of being conceived out of sight, subconscious seeds that germinate slowly, almost stealthily, until they penetrate the surface, taking up so much space that it becomes necessary to take them into account. In the process, many people, wittingly and unwittingly, contribute to their final unfolding. It is impossible, therefore, to identify everyone who is due my thanks, but particular gratitude is owed to those who spurred, suggested, and shared with me their specific expertise during the writing of this book, and these are: Mike Hyman at Collca, for useful insights into the publishing industry; Lorraine Mace, my ever eagle-eyed and perceptive editor, and Nichola Meyer, Founder and Principal of the NZ, SA, and UK Writers' Colleges. Any errors, of course, are my own.

Appendices

Useful Websites and Books:

Websites:

Because web addresses may become out of date, I have included here only a small number of well-established sites. Whenever you access them, you will find up-to-date links to other sites and articles as new material is posted.

Reference sources on words, grammar and syntax –

Online English Grammar (British English)
www.edufind.com/english/grammar/index.cfm
Daily Writing Tips (American English)
http://www.dailywritingtips.com/category/grammar/
Online Etymology Dictionary
http://www.etymonline.com/index

Indexing services (societies of indexers) –

UK: http://www.indexers.org.uk/
USA: http://www.asindexing.org/
Australia and NZ: http://anzsi.org/site/

Information and directories on all aspects of publishing and writing –

International ISBN Agency (Information about ISBNs and how they operate in
different countries)
http://www.isbn-international.org/agency
(From the link below, select any country to find its national ISBN agency)

http://www.isbn-international.org/agency

Publishing Perspectives (An online magazine of international news and opinion on books and publishing)
http://publishingperspectives.com

Write Words (UK-based online writing community offering advice, information, and a directory page including nonfiction publishers and agents)
http://www.writewords.org.uk/directory/

Publishers Global (Website of international news for the publishing industry as well as authors, includes a directory of publishers and publishing services sorted by country, subject, language and city)
www.publishersglobal.com

Publishers Association of South Africa (directory of members from where you can search for 'non-fiction publishers', and advice and information about publishing)
http://www.publishsa.co.za/members-andfreelancers/members/publishers/list

The Book Doctor (A directory of Australian nonfiction publishers sorted by genres)
www.bookdoctor.com.au/nonfiction.html

Publishers Weekly (Weekly news magazine about international publishing, targeting authors and agents as well as publishers, book sellers and librarians. Requires a subscription for full access to the site)
www.publishersweekly.com

Writers Services (Website offering free information and advice for traditional and self-publishing authors)
www.WritersServices.com

You Write On (UK-based online writing community providing peer review, tips, resources and opportunities for professional feedback through its Arts Council of England sponsorship)
www.youwriteon.com

The Independent Publishing Magazine (online magazine edited by Mick Rooney, providing tips and articles about self-publishing)
http://www.theindependentpublishingmagazine.com/

Publishing Services Index (reviews and rankings of publishing services, an index provided in the above online magazine)
http://www.theindependentpublishingmagazine.com/p/publishing-ser.html

The Alliance of Independent Authors (ALLi) (a non-profit membership organisation for self-publishing authors, based in UK but with world-wide membership, whose website offers information, resources, and guidance on reputable self-publishing service providers)
http://allianceindependentauthors.org/

Writing blogs –

Blogs about writing nonfiction vary in their approach, some focus more on short-form journalism than writing books, and new ones come online all the time. To find sites that suit your particular interests, enter 'nonfiction writing blogs' in an online search – 'creative nonfiction' brings up a slightly different list but there is some overlap – or add a topic such as 'travel' or 'memoir' to your search terms.

Crowd-funding sites –

Unbound (UK-based site for authors)
http://unbound.co.uk/
Kickstarter (international site for a range of creative endeavours)
http://www.kickstarter.com/
Publush Foundation (international site for authors which pursues a cause to improve child literacy)
http://www.pubslush.com/

General research resources –

Project Gutenberg (Vast source of free material especially in literature, art and history)
www.gutenberg.org/
The Public Domain Review (Online journal of the Open Knowledge Foundation giving free public access to a wide range of books and documents as they come out of copyright)
http://publicdomainreview.org/
The British Library (This link is to their page for assisting researchers)
http://www.bl.uk/reshelp/index.html

Sites that monitor feedback on publishes and agents, and issue warnings –

Writer Beware
  http://www.sfwa.org/other-resources/for-authors/writer-beware/
Editors and Predators (Also provides advice and tips on making submissions, and lists links to writers' resources)
  http://pred-ed.com/

Writers' associations –

Writers' and authors' associations, societies and guilds are too numerous to list, but are present in most countries at national and regional levels; some specialise in nonfiction, or even on a specific genre. You can find what is available in your area through an online search, through your social media contacts, or by asking at a local library.

Books:

Ackroyd, Peter (2002) *Dickens*, Vintage [Quote: *'To find in a day, a moment…* ' Prologue p. xv]

Baverstock, A. (2007) *Marketing Your Book, an Author's Guide*, A&C Black Ltd

Bryson, Bill (2008 revised edition) *Bryson's Dictionary for Writers and Editors*, Doubleday [Handy reference for words, spellings, grammar and facts that often catch us out]

Galley, Ben and **Mick Rooney** (2013 an ebook) *Choosing a Self Publishing Service 2013: The Alliance of Independent Authors Guide,* Font Publications [in addition to a detailed comparison of twenty service providers, the book contains general information on self-publishing with a range of methods and collaborations]

Hoole, Gavin and **Cheryl Smith** (2006) *Really, Really, Really Easy Step-by-Step Digital Photography* (New Holland)

New Zealand Writer's Handbook (5th edition), Bateman

Orwell, George (1984) *The Penguin Essays of George Orwell*, Penguin [Quote: *'the right to report contemporary events truthfully…'* in 'The Prevention of Literature' p.336]

Truss, Lynne (2009) *Eats, Shoots and Leaves*, Fourth Estate [A humorous but deadly serious guide to punctuation]

Writers' & Artists' Yearbook (updated annually), A&C Black Ltd [a 'Bible' on all matters of writing and publishing for UK writers]

Nonfiction books quoted as examples:

Travel –

Deep Sea and Foreign Going: Inside Shipping, the Invisible Industry that Brings You 90% of Everything, Rose George (Portobello 2013)

From Heaven Lake. Travels through Sikiang and Tibet, Vikram Seth (Abacus 1984)

The Old Patagonia Express: By Train Through the Americas, Paul Theroux (Mariner Books 1989)

The Songlines, Bruce Chatwin (Picador1987)

Two Wings of a Nightingale: Persian soul. Islamic heart, Jill Worrall (Exisle 2011)

History –

What Jane Austen Ate and Charles Dickens Knew, Daniel Pool (Touchstone 1993)

The Invention of Murder, Judith Flanders (Harper Press 2011)

Medieval Lives, Terry Jones and Alan Eriera (BBC Books 2004)

The History of Tibet: Conversations with the Dalai Lama, Thomas Laird (Atlantic Books 2006)

Biography –

The Poets' Daughters: Dora Wordsworth and Sara Coleridge, Katie Waldegrave (Hutchinson 2013)

Poe: a Life Cut Short, Peter Ackroyd (Vintage 2009)

The Bookseller of Kabul, Asne Seierstad (Virago 2002)

Gaudi: a biography, Gijs van Hensbergen (Perennial 2003)

Einstein: His Life and Universe, Walter Isaacson (Pocket Books 2008)

Memoir and autobiography –

Mongol, Uuganaa Ramsay (Saraband Books 2014)

Somewhere Near the End, Diana Athill (Granta 2009)

Ammonites and Leaping Fish: A Life in Time, Penelope Lively (Fig Tree 2013)

Afrika My Music, Es'kia Mphahlele (First published 1985 by Ravan Press. Published by Kwela Books 2014)

Self-help and how-to books –

How to Get a Grip: (Forget Namby-Pamby, Wishy Washy, Self-Help Drivel. This is the Book You Need), Matthew Kimberley (Ad Lib 2011)

The Society of Timid Souls: Or, How to be Brave, Polly Morland (Profile Books 2013)

The longest Journey: Finding the True Self, Amanda Stuart (Sid Harta 2012)

Tie-dye: Dye it, Wear it, Share it, Shabd Simon-Alexander (Potter Craft 2013)

Kaikai Aniani, R. J. May (Robert Brown and Associates 1984)

The New Artisan Bread in Five Minutes a Day: The Discovery That Revolutionizes Home Baking, Jeff Hertzberg, Zoë François and Stephen Scott Gross (Thomas Dunne Books, revised edition 2013)

Feed the Family for $15 or Less, Sophie Gray ((Random House NZ 2012)

The Kiwi Backyard Handbook, Justin Newcombe (Penguin Group NZ 2011)

Educational and text books, and documentaries –

Outdoor Classrooms: A Handbook for School Gardens, Carolyn Nuttall and Janet Millington (Permanent Publications 2013)

17 Equations that Changed the World, Ian Stewart (Profile Books 2013)

Floating City: Hustlers, Strivers, Dealers, Call Girls and Other Lives in Illicit New York, Sudhir Venkatesh (Allen Lane 2013)

Johannes Gutenberg and the Printing Press, Diana Childress (Twenty-First Century Books 2008)

The Age of Consent, George Monbiot (Harper Perennial 2004)

Conversations with My Sons and Daughters, Mamphela Ramphele (Penguin Global 2013)

Glossary of Common Writing, Printing and Publishing Terms

This list is not intended to be exhaustive. It focuses on terms employed in this book and those that you might find in general reading on these topics.

Acknowledgements: 1. author's statement thanking others for ideas, information etc **2.** recognition of permissions granted to use copyright material (which should be specified)

Acquisition: negotiating process by which a publisher buys rights in a book

Advance: payment to a writer which is set against royalties earned after a book is published

Appendix/ces: supporting information at the end of a book e.g. glossary, historical timeline

Artwork: illustrations for publication including photographs, tables and other graphics

Author Publicity Form (APF): publisher's form for authors to detail their potential to contribute to marketing and publicity

Back-cover copy: information provided on the back of a printed book

Backlist: books published in previous years and still in print/selling

Backmatter: (see **End pages**)

Backstory: events that occurred before the story/narrative presently being told, which may be revealed gradually as the narrative unfolds

Binding: the joining of pages to construct a book by gluing, stitching or stapling

Bio: 'author biography' – a brief résumé to establish the credibility of an author

Blurb: brief description of a book and/or its author on the back cover (as 'back-cover copy') of a book and elsewhere as publicity material

Content: text and images as applied to web pages, blogs and other online locations

Conversion: changing a document file into a format suitable for digital reading devices or for printing

Copy: text intended for publication, especially in newspapers, magazines etc

Copy-edit: (also **line-by-line edit**) detailed scrutiny of a manuscript/typescript to correct errors of grammar, syntax, and fact

Copyright: the exclusive right to use, assign, or sell original material by the person/entity who created it in accordance with the Universal Copyright Convention (UCC)

Cover letter: brief letter accompanying a submission to a publisher

Creative nonfiction (CNF): factual account written with the creative writing techniques of storytelling. In the USA the author's personal experience is generally central to the narrative

Download: electronically transfer files from one source e.g. a web page, to another such as a personal computer by purchase or for free e.g. software programmes, ebooks, articles

DRM (Digital Rights Management): a method of formatting digital text intended to prevent unauthorised copying or pirating

Ebook: a book of text and/or images that can be read on an electronic reading device

End pages (endmatter: (in USA **backmatter)** pages after the main text in a book e.g. bibliography, appendices, notes

Epigraph: relevant quotation at the front of a book on a separate page, or quotations at the start of each chapter

Epilogue: in a book, an additional, concluding text immediately after the final chapter

Extent: total number of pages in a book

Flashback: description of a past event that happened before the present story being related

Flash forward: piece of text in a narrative that indicates some future event or outcome

Foldout (gatefold): a folded book page that opens out e.g. to show a map or family tree

Font: distinctive design-set of characters for printing text ('typeface' before digital printing)

Foreword: statement before the main text of a book endorsing the author and/or content

Format: 1. Shape and size of a printed book **2.** Arrangement of data for storage/retrieval in digital form

Formatting: in electronic publishing, arranging data to be read on various digital devices

Frontispiece: an illustration located before the main text of a book

Frontlist: books recently, or soon to be, published

Frontmatter: (see **preliminary pages**)

Genre: type or style of writing, or of a book e.g. fiction, nonfiction, also applied to subject categories such as biography, travel, health etc

Gutter: inside margins of book pages, usually wider than outer margins to allow for binding

Hashtag: in social media, the character # attached to a word to attract searches

Header: information printed in the top margin of a page, called a 'running header' when repeated on every page of a chapter or book

Hi-res: high resolution image in photography required for quality printing (see also TIFF)

Hook: opening lines of a text that grabs attention, encouraging a reading to continue

House style: grammar, spelling and punctuation options preferred by a particular publisher

Hyperlink: an active/clickable link taking the reader to another part of a document ('internal'), or to another place such as a website ('external')

Imagery: language that appeals to readers' senses, especially by using metaphor and simile

Imprint: 1. Brand name under which a company publishes a book **2.** Publishers' details printed on the title/copyright page of a book

Independent: 1. Publisher of any size not owned or controlled by another company (e.g. not an imprint of a larger entity) **2.** Author who publishes his/her own work, with or without hired technical assistance. In both cases, applied to widely differing arrangements and not a precise term with a single meaning

ISBN (International Standard Book Number): numerical identity required for each edition of a published work for it to be distributed and retailed, issued by a specific national agency in each country

Jpeg (.jpg): file format for storing images in a compressed form for digital transmission or on web pages (not usually in high enough resolution for quality printing)

Justified: text spaced to extend evenly between left and right margins

Layout: arrangement of text, illustrations, margins etc in the design of a book, magazine, or other media

Left aligned: text flush to the left margin leaving uneven line lengths on the right

Location: in an ebook, a numerical identifier for a block of text on a digital reading device (i.e. in relation to the screen, instead of page number as in a printed book)

Look-Inside: feature in online bookstores allowing browsers to read sections of a book

Mainstream: an imprecise term applied loosely to describe well-established, principal companies in publishing and the media

Metaphor: a word or phrase replacing a factual description of an object, scene or action with an imagined or alternative identity to provide new insights into the original meaning

MS/ms: manuscript, text document (interchangeable with 'typescript')

Narrative nonfiction: factual account expressed in the creative writing style of storytelling

Orphan: printing term for a first line of text separated from its paragraph by a page break

Outline: a plan summarising a proposed book or article

Pagination: the printing of numbers on the pages of a book

PDF (.pdf): Portable Document Format, an electronic file format used for printing, and also for reading documents on computers

PerfectBound: a book's pages bound (more cheaply) with glue as opposed to stapling or stitching

Permissions: procedure for asking (and possibly paying for) authority to quote/use text or artwork copyrighted or published by someone else

Plate: separate page in a print book bearing an illustration or other special information

POD: print on demand, a digital-based system which can produce small quantities of printed works cost-effectively

Point of view: the perspective from which a narrative is written e.g. as if telling one's own story ('first person'), or describing another person's actions ('third person')

Preface: statement by the author at the beginning of a book to inform readers about its scope or background

Preliminary pages (front pages): (in USA **frontmatter**) pages before the main text of a book e.g. title page, copyright notice, table of contents, often numbered in roman numerals

Printing: 1. Lithographic printing – chemical-based process for printing from metal plates (cylinders). **2.** Digital printing – electronic-based process for printing from digital files, as used for print on demand

Print-ready copy: finished text or artwork in a suitable form for printing or publishing

Print run: number of books printed in one order

Product description: brief description of a book listed in online bookstores (see also 'blurb')

Prologue: a piece of writing before the main text of a book to create a mood or setting, used more in fiction than nonfiction works

Proof: trial-printed document for checking and correcting before publication

Proofreading marks: standardised symbols to indicate corrections on a proof

Proposal: concise description of the purpose, potential readers, marketability and contents of a manuscript as part of a submission to a publisher or agent

Query: author's approach to an agent with a request to be represented by him/her

Recto: right-hand page of an opened book (bearing odd numbers); (verso: left-hand bearing even numbers)

Release date: the date a publisher instructs its distributor to release a book from the warehouse to bookstores (may pre-date the official publication date)

Remaindered: status of unsold new books when returned by a bookseller to the publisher

Reversion (of rights): process whereby the rights to publish copyright material are relinquished by a publisher and returned to the author

Rights: the rights to publish copyright material in various forms and territories assigned by the author to a publishing company, usually for an agreed number of years

Royalty: the percentage of revenue that authors receive from a publisher on the sale of their books

Simile: a phrase or word describing an object, action, place or person as being 'like' something else

Structural editing: review and correction of a manuscript for structure, flow, logicality and completeness

Style: 1. amalgamation of syntax, word usage, tone and structure in recognisable forms (e.g. 'formal', 'popular') **2.** Distinctive combinations of these that characterise the work of a particular author

Submission: the process of sending specified documents to a publisher or agent in application to be published, or represented, respectively

Subsidiary rights (subrights): rights assigned by an author enabling a publisher to pursue additional forms of publication e.g. audio books, digital editions, translations

Synopsis: brief, concise rendering of a text to show its most significant features and style, used for submissions and various forms of publicity

Tag-line: short phrase that captures the principle feature or appeal of a 'story', used in headlines, social media and other promotion

Text: the main body of a work distinct from preface, appendices, illustrations etc

Theme: an over-arching idea or message that runs through a narrative giving it cohesion and purpose

TIFF (.tif): Tagged Image File Format, digital format for storing images at high resolution and used for high quality printing

Timeline: chronological list of events, or sequence of actions

ToC: Table of Contents at the beginning of a book or document

Trade publishing: books produced for general readers, or the popular market, rather than specialist markets such as text books

TS/ts: typescript, document of typed text (used interchangeably with 'manuscript')

Typo: typing error

Upload: transfer files/information from a computer or other electronic device to a website, or to some other facility on the Internet for use or storage

URL: Universal Resource Locator, a web address or other specific location on the Internet

Verso: left-hand page of an opened book (bearing even numbers); (recto: right-hand page bearing odd numbers)

Voice: combination of syntax, word choices etc that distinguishes one writer from another

Whitespace: parts of a book page without text e.g. margins, line spaces

Widow: printer's term for a word or phrase appearing alone at the top of a page because of the previous page break

Word count: total number of words in a document or manuscript

About the author:

Dr Trish Nicholson has 30 years of writing experience, as columnist, feature writer, and author of narrative nonfiction and prize-winning short stories. Among her published works are books on human resource management, social anthropology, and responsible travel. Recent titles include eBooks of travelogue, popular science and creative writing craft, and the paperback edition of *Inside Stories for Writers and Readers*.

Starting with a degree in social anthropology and a first career in regional government in Europe and the UK, where she was also a tutor in the Open University and the Open Business School, Trish moved into management training before taking her skills overseas. After 5 years working in the West Sepik province of Papua New Guinea on a World Bank development project, she spent 3 years in the Philippines running the volunteer programme for VSO (Voluntary Service Overseas). A grant from the UK Department for International Development enabled her to follow this with research into tourism initiatives by indigenous communities in the Philippines, Vietnam, and Australia.

After travelling and working in over twenty countries, Trish now lives in New Zealand, combining her passions for writing narrative nonfiction, storytelling and photography, spending as much time as she can in her tree house. You can follow her on Twitter as @trishanicholson and visit her website – Trish Nicholsons Words in the Treehouse – www.trishnicholsonswordsinthetreehouse.com

Other recent titles by Trish Nicholson (published by Collca):

Narrative non-fiction writing:

Writing Your Nonfiction Book is also available in a digital edition. Details and suppliers are given on Collca's webpage:

http://collca.com/wynb

Creative writing:

Inside Stories for Writers and Readers – a companion and creative writing resource for teachers as well as a personal mentor, it contains also 15 of the author's original stories, analysed and critiqued. The paperback edition includes *From Apes to Apps: How Humans Evolved as Storytellers and Why it Matters.*

Popular science:

From Apes to Apps: How Humans Evolved as Storytellers and Why it Matters – a cautionary tale drawing on recent research in neuroscience, psychology, archaeology, biology, linguistics, and the author's own field, anthropology, revealing the fact that our brain function is based on narrative – stories – and why this makes us vulnerable in the digital age.

Travelogue:

Journey in Bhutan: Himalayan Trek in the Kingdom of the Thunder Dragon –

a detailed personal account sharing the experience of the extraordinary landscape, culture and heritage of this 'hidden' Buddhist Kingdom, an eBook lavishly illustrated with 37 full colour plates of the author's own photographs. Appendices include a historical timeline, glossary, and survival guide to Bhutanese Buddhism.

Travel-ethnography:

Masks of the Moryons: Easter Week in Mogpog – the only published narrative of the spectacular Easter Week celebrations in the Philippine island of Marinduque re-enacting the Legend of Longinus and Crucifixion of Jesus of Nazareth. A case-study of culture and tourism, the eBook contains 28 of the author's original colour plates of rituals, masks, processions and portrayals, a glossary, and study notes on cultural tourism.

For further information about any of these eBooks, please access this page on Collca's website:

http://collca.com/TrishNicholson